ECONOMIC EMPOWERMENT OF WOMEN

ECONOMIC EMPOWERMENT OF WOMEN

By

Dr. Rajib Lochan Panigrahy

&

Dr. Sudhansu Sekhar Nayak

DISCOVERY PUBLISHING HOUSE PVT. LTD.

NEW DELHI-110 002

First Published-2008
Reprinted-2011

ISBN: 978-81-8356-332-1

Published by:

DISCOVERY PUBLISHING HOUSE PVT. LTD.

4831/24, Ansari Road, Prahlad Street,
Darya Ganj, New Delhi-110 002 (India)
Phone: 23279245 • Fax: 91-11-23253475
E-mail: dphbooks@radiffmail.com
dphtemp@indiatimes.com
Website: www.discoverypublishinghouse.com

Printed at:
Mehra Offset Press, Delhi.

Preface

Women empowerment is an age-old concept. In the past centuries women are empowered in society. In the pace of time, in the changing scenario, in the changing economy and increasing population, Government formulated certain plans, policies, schemes to make the women healthier, wealthier. There are special acts articulated for them and seminars, conferences organized to analyse, task forces organised to trace the activities, utilisations and improvements held. The women empowerment is a concept to improvise the economic status of women specially in less developed countries and in every part of globe in whole. It is also made to reduce the gender inequalities, to increase social status of women. When the economic status of an women increases, education and awareness increases side-by-side and they tries to improve it, than the status and gender inequality automatically increases. From the articles we find women are honest in work and fulfils the aim and objectives of scheme and jobs given to them. In India most of the schemes and funds not reaching to them and few have such administrative and operative discrepancies, which cannot fulfil their goals. Hence, is a need of implementation of schemes for women empowerment, which should reach them in proper manner, so that the women empowerment will fulfil the aims and objects.

R.L. Panigrahy
S.S. Nayak

Acknowledgements

We are very much thankful to all paper contributors of this book, it is not possible on our part to edit this book without their kind help and cooperation.

We would like to express our regards to our parents and family members for their encouragement for writing and preparation of the book completed. They also encouraged for writing research topics.

We have to express our gratitude to our teacher, guide and elders by whose blessings we can complete the work and see the daylight.

Finally, we have very much thankful and grateful to Shri Tilak Wasan, Proprietor, Discovery Publishing House, New Delhi who had readily accepted our proposal for publishing this book in spite of his heavy pressure during this session. We, on behalf of all paper contributors, family members and friends, very much thankful to all staff members of Discovery Publishing House for their kind help and co-operation provided by them in publishing this book in time.

R.L. Panigrahy
S.S. Nayak

Contents

1

Changing the Dimensions of Women Towards Challenging Future

*Dr. Bandana Gaur**

In Indian society, women's status has always remained high theoretically powers of God have been described in women's forms as Laxmi, Sarsasati, Durga etc. Thus women has been considered a symbol of wealth, knowledge and strength. Wife has been called 'Ardliangini' (half part of body) and motherhood has also been given a great respect. Mother is the symbol of Nationality also, which gives us impression of women's status, higher than men's status.

Practically, although during various periods certain ups and downs in it were visible from the archaeological remnants the vedic literature we get indication of women's status in comparison to men's status being higher and same, respectively during pre-vedic and vedic periods. But from post-vedic period its downward flow of gradual deterioration started and continued till the end of medieval period and the women quietly suffered throughout. In British period there are several reforms made up by reformers and several laws were enacted.

---

*Bandana Gaur Sr. Lecturer Department Sociology Faculty Social Sciences Dayalbagh Educational Institute, Dayalbagh, Agra.

In independent India for more improvement of women's status, welfare policy was formulated and various programmes were chalked out. Indian constitutions guarantees full equality between the man and women. Government is very active in all the main directions, i.e., health, education occupation welfare etc.

United Nations Organizations first declared 1975 as international women's year and later on declared the period 1975-85, as women's decade, during which is the whole world welfare of women was discussed, policies were changed, new programmes were adopted and women study centres were established.

Socio-Cultural Dimension

Under the dimension of socio-cultural the status of female members of the family as a daughter, daughter-in-law-wife mother housewife, as a working women and serious thought is given to the institution of marriage. In the socio-cultural dimension the women mobility and freedom outside the house is considered opportunity of interaction and interrelationship with outside people, specially the males, and its usage, free outside movements for various reasons, organization of women's association and friends society or group and participation in their activities etc.

Several laws have been passed to improve the condition of women. The Hindu Marriage Act has prohibited polygamy. Laws have also been made to make divorce more easily available. Women are today entitled to equal share in their parental property. In the sphere of employment, law ensures equal wages for equal to both men and women. Women are gradually becoming aware their rights and their role in the society.

Under social status of women their freedom and mobility out a residence in considered. In the modern period, women of the middle class in cities work work-field was limited upto the four walls of the house, go out of the house for education and occupation. They have also got the freedom of conversation with out side males, if required. They move out of their homes with full freedom even during night time, and entertain themselves with friend. They can go anywhere, come back at any time and live alone anywhere. Women of upper class also remain out of house till late rights for entertainment but with their husbands or escorts, although during day time they are free to move either alone or with, friends for some jobs or entertainment. In rural society, in lower class less, but in middle and upper classes more, restrictions have been imposed on their freedom of movement.

In this way women are giving challenges in socio-cultural dimensions.

Economic Dimension

Women remain financially dependent therefore they are explained. This can be considered as the non-acceptance of human rights and non-availability of social justice for them. Opposite to this from economic independence, economic base for the freedom of women gets prepared which later on opens the path of social freedom and getting rid of salavery of men becomes possible for them. New thoughts, knowledge of rights and duties in themselves are quite encouraging for the development of their personality there social and creative powers are utilized not only for them but for the progress of society also. Therefore this is the basic principle of United Nations. In Organization's declaration that discrimination against women should be finished. Therefore, they should get opportunities and equal rights of economic participation in the society which is quite necessary for the improvement of their status.

Under this aspect, women's right's on familiar property thinking about 'Stridhan' (ownership of movable properly) personal income and economic independence, etc. are considered. By law the right of getting a share equal to the heirs is family property, has been given to them. On stridhan women has got the full ownership right, which no person can use against her wishes.

Economic empowerment has two aspect. One is income or livelihood. The other is whether or not women have effective control over this income or livelihood. The parameters of economic empowerment of women are.

- Educate and motivate women to undertake income generating activities.
- Provide information and knowledge on various self employment and income generating activities.
- Mobilize women to form self-help Group.
- Encourage savings and utilize it for further income generation.
- Identifying local skills and utilize these skills in income generation and self employment activities.
- Create income generating activities.
- Provide access to support services.
- Provide financial assistance.
- Provide technical assistance.
- Develop managerial capabilities.
- Encourage entrepreneurship
- Provide training on innovative technologies.
- Give emphasis on improving women's control over material resource and strengthening economic security.
- Ensure equal wages for equal work.

Policies Advocated Women's Concerns

Government has been conscious to have an enabling policy environment in which women's concerns are reflected, articulated and redressed by the Government, the voluntary and corporate world. The National Commission on women was set up in 1992 to review the existing laws related to women, suggest amendments whereever necessary and look into the complaints involving deprivation of the rights of women. As a follow up of the commitment made by India in the fourth world conference of women held at Beijing in September 1995, a draft of a National Comprehensive Policy for empowerment of women has been prepared for adoption. The policy is envisaged to direct strategies and action in all sections of government activity, to achieve advancement and empowerment of women and eliminate discriminations.

The Indira Mahila Yojana (IMY) launched in 1995 aims at co-ordinating and integrating sectoral programmes relevant to women like health, education, water, sanitations, housing and others at local block and district levels and increasing their awareness and income through group activities and participation with the aim of empowering women. Indira Mahila Kendra would be established at village level and Indira Mahila Block Kendras at Block level for this purpose. The programme would be a centrally sponsored scheme. Non-Government organizations would also be involved in this process.

The Eight Plan (1992-97) laid special thrust on employment, including women's employment with the objective to make women self-reliant and economically independent. The major programmes is this regard are the poverty alleviations programmes of IRDP and TRYSEM where is there are stipulations that 40 per cent of the benefits should go to women. In wage employment programme of Jawahar Rozgar Yojana up to 30 per cent benefits have been reserved for women. These programmes are implemented by Department of Rural Development and Poverty Alleviations. The Department of Women and Child Development launched the programme of support to training and employment on a sustainable basis in the traditional sectors of agriculture, dairying, fisheries, sericulture, handlooms etc. The NORAD assited programme of Training-cum-employment-cum-production centers, trained women in non-traditional and uncommon trades such as electronics, computers, printing, beauty culture etc., to give sustainable employment to women. The Socio-Economic Programme implemented by Central Social Welfare Boards provides work and wages to needy women. Such as destitute, widows, deserted and economically backward and handicapped. These programmes have benefited more than 11 lacks women. Rashtriya Mahila Kosh is the most significant intervention launched in 1993, with the objectives of meeting the credit needs of poor, asset less women, mostly is the form section.

The programme for Development of Women is Rural Areas (DWCRA), launched is 1982-83, inaugurated an era for systematically organizing women is groups for enhancing their earning on self-sustainable basis and increasing their access to and utilizations of services like health, child care and adult education, among others. The programme called for formation groups of 10-15 women who would collectively engage in an activity. A revolving fund of Rs. 15,000 (Presently enhanced to Rs. 25,000) was made available to each group for credit and administrative needs. Supplementing of staff by inclusion of an additional Gram Sevika and appointment of a lady officer to the post of Assistant Project Officer to oversee implementation to the programme were called for subsequently with a view to fortifying the programme further and increasing awareness and community based convergent services (CBCS) component and information, education and communication (IEC) component were included. The Department of Women and Child Department has been implementing the programme for hostels for working women from 1973. The scheme of crèches for children of working mothers, provide creches services to the children of poor working women in enabling them to pursue employment. A National Creche fund has been set up in March 1993, to meet the growing demand for crèches.

Women of today have been taken up jobs in every front defence, police, pilot and industrialist. Whatever field we can think women has manage prove herself. They are being recognized by the world as equivalent to men in almost all occupations fields.

Political Dimension: It is undying fact that women played a very crucial role in our freedom struggle. When India got its independence several women leaders occupied prominent positives and the constitution give them equal rights and legitionised their role for participation. Along with participation of a large number of women on the freedom movement efforts of Gandhiji, had direct-influence on the section of political and social elites in which their female family members were also included. In 1925 Sarojini Naidu become president of Indian National Congress and provided Leadership to the women liberating movement in 1930, in one meeting of representative women organizations, immediate acceptance of franchise without any discriminations between man and women, was demanded. In 1931 women got right of candidature in elections with certain condition in eligibility. Those conditions were definite amount of property should be on the name of women and she should be graduate for 7 years prior to election which means that only the educated and rich women were given this right. Due to these terms and conditions almost all women got deprived of this right because in India very few, even educated women, have property on their names. In 1931 itself Indian National Congress declared the provision of all types of rights to all the citizen without any discrimination. Gradually women understood importance of their life, examined their capabilities realized their duty of struggling themselves to safeguard their interests, made organization more powerful and forwarded their demands. Now they have to achieve rights equal to men in every field of life which they received in 1947 with political right at central level. On this bases it was obvious to get equal opportunities without any discriminations of sex, in other areas also. From this women got the right of influencing the parliament not only for their own interests but they could also get changed or formed policies connected with political, economic and cultural fields affecting the whole country.

Franchise for women meant their recognition and responsibility in taking decision regarding national life. It also meant that they are not inferior to men and if they get freedom and opportunity, they can take and property handle the challenging job and responsibilities of positions like ministers, governors ambassadors etc.

In changing time the establishment of a national commission to monitor the status of women, reservation of 33 per cent of seats in the village Panchayats (councils) through a constitutional amendment and the measures being contemplated to reserve 33 per cent of seats for women in the parliament and the state assemblies testify to the increasing recognition of the role of women in the power structure of our society.

The Panchayati Raj Institutions are the prime movers of decentralization of the grassroots level the main aim of Panchayati Raj Institution is to accelerate the pace of development and involve all segments of populations in the process so that their needs and aspiration can be fulfilled the participation of women in these bodies ensures efficient equitable and sustainable community oriented development. Their involvement provides them opportunity, autonomy and freedom to decide for themselves. However the participation of women in the political process has been severely limited.

Conclusion

The need of the hour is to create an environment which ensure dignity to the women of today have taken up jobs in every front defense, police, pilot and industrialist whatever field we can think of, woman has managed to prove herself. They are being recognized by the world as equivalent to men in almost all occupational field. As the women has been empowered with right to property and divorce as well as freedom of marriage she has ample opportunities to improve her overall status intelligently. The women has full rights in terms of education of her children family management and religious etc. It clarifies that the vigorous changes have cracked down the age old suppression and repression of Indian women. Finally, we can say that it has been rightly said that "Earth's noblest thing, a women perfected". Next to god we are indebted to women first for life itself then for making it worth living.

REFERENCES

1. Panigrahi Kumar Santosh, "Status of women in India during era of Globalization", *Third Concept International Journal,* February 2005.
2. Mishra Sarswati, *Status of Women,* p. 10.
3. Singh Yogendra, "Culture Change in India", *Identity and Globalization,* p. 125.
4. Dr. Das Rani Sandhya, *Empowerment of Women,* "A Holistic Approach" Third Concept, An International Journals of Ideas.
5. Sahay Sushama, *Women and Empowerment—Approaches and Strategies,* Discovery Publishing House, New Delhi 1998.
6. Mitra Moinak & Chatterjee Baslesi Moumita, Times for India inc to Women "Breaking the Glass Ceiling is Still a Far Crying for Women Executives", *The Economic Times,* New Delhi Thursday, 8 March 2007.
7. Hazarika Anjali, "The New Road to the Top", *The Economic Times,* New Delhi, Thursday, 8 March 2007.
8. Bijapurkar, Igniting Women Entrepreneurship, *The Economic Times,* New Delhi, Thursday, 8 March 2007.
9. Dr. Singh Indrabhusan and Dr. Km., Usha, "Rural and Women Empowerment," *Kurukshetra* March 2007 a Journal on Rural Development
10. Anderson, M.L. 1988, *Thinking about Women, Sociological Feminist Perspectives,* 2nd edition, New York: Macmillan.
11. Bandura, Albert 1986, *Social Foundation of Thought,* Englewood Cliffs, N.J. Prentice-Hall.

2

Women Partners in Development

Dr. Padma Charana Padhi

Women thy name is Creation. The undivided Car and attention for a period of nine month and nine days have enabled women to nature life within them. So as to maintain the spontaneity or the human civilization.

"When women moves forward the family moves the village moves and the nation moves". These words of Pandit Jawaharlal Nehru is the central theme in the Socio-Economic Paradigm of the country as it is an accepted fact that only when women are in the main stream of progress can any economic and social development be meaningful. Agriculture is the mainstay of Indian economy as over 70 per cent of Indian Population depend upon agriculture and allied occupation for their livelihood. The rural women often called as "farmwomen" constitute almost 50 per cent of farm work force and play a significant role in Indian agriculture. The present inflationary pressures warrant women to join the male member of the family for securing a substantial livelihood. Women have come out from the traditionally patterned society and associated with the professional society for gaining economic independence and creating the same for others by taking up self-empowerment venture.

Women undertake various types of farm operation along with men in this society and county. To access their significant contribution to agriculture. Some allied operations like livestock, forestry etc. needs to be considered as well. The role of farm women can be broadly classified under three broad categories:

(1) Paid labourers. (2) Cultivators when they work in their own land as unpaid labourer. (3) Mangers of certain aspects of agricultural production.

When pages of history were scanned it was revealed that women are the pioneers of farming. It was women who first domesticated the crop plants and there by the art and science of the farming.

While men went out hunting for food, women gathered seeds from the flora and began cultivation for needs of food, fodder, fiber and fuel. Thus women have an umbilical attachment with agriculture since time immemorial.

Food Production

Women are involved in every stage of food production. Sustainable food security is a mandate of all households to ensure both physical and economic access to a balanced diet, pre-sowing operations like puddling seed selection and treatment nursery bed raising, transplanting seedling, thinning and gap filling are some of the activities where women play an active role. After securing of different field crops, they do weeding and hoeing, scaring of birds filling of spray equipment with pesticide solution for effective crop husbandry. Harvesting and post harvesting also engage a considerable amount of farm women in various chores like threshing and winnowing digging of groundnuts and potatoes, tea leaf and vegetable picking, processing and storages. However the post harvests functions varies with purpose and location. Keeping in view the traditional knowledge, and skill of firmwomen in different farm operation, it will not be wise to ignore the possibility of increasing avenues, which will uphold the country food status through utilization of this unattended and unrecognized power.

Dairy and Livestock

The female sector of countries human resources play a significant role in dairing activities like milking, fodder cutting, cleaning cattle and cattle shed, preparation and storage of cow dung cakes etc. livestock contributes 25 per cent of the total income of the agriculture sector.

In addition women play an equally important role in decision-making regarding number of milch cattle to be kept, purchase of cattle feed and place of keeping animals in summer, winter.

In spite of their major role in dairying activities majority of the farm women get information from their surrounding and form any institutional sources, as they are being left out form extension programmes related to animal husbandry.

Poultry

Among agricultural operations poultry farming gives the highest return per unit of land used. Moreover it is not dependent on the monsoon or irrigation and can successfully utilized dry lands, which might other wise, remain idle. Feeding and watering of the birds, collection of eggs and marketing are some key management practices carried out by the women. However lack of technical training, poor cash management and marketing facilities are the major bottlenecks for the successful carrying out of this activity. Development of new market through rural-urban linkages and maintenances of hygiene in poultry houses are the mandacts to get high returns which adds to the family income of the farmer.

Aquaculture

Aquaculture opens up new vistas of economic progress for rural women. It can be practiced as extra occupation simultaneously with any others traditional vocation. When it is taken up in combination with horticulture or even poultry, broad, basing of economic activities nearer home and within the purview of the women folk occurs, even small backyard ponds can be turned into successful resources basis with the use of appropriate aquaculture technology. The same pond can be utilized for fry and fingerling being rearing and table sized fish production. The more progressive women participants have mastered the breeding technique of the common corp. The spawn produced is a good source of income and provides the starting material for fry production. Lack of adequate supply of feeds is a major constraint and if women are trained to prepare the feed at the village level it will provide new employment opportunities.

Women show great skill in fishing net fabrication, which is used as an indoor income generating activity.

Food Processing

The chain from farmer to consumer is long and often complicated women's work along this food chain does not end with cultivating crops. But they are also responsible for processing, preserving and storing the food so that it is safe, nutritious and available through out the year. Transforming paddy, into rice by milling, making puffed rice, drying fish, cleaning and slicing fruits and vegetables for canning are some of the processing activities where women have a major share of labour. In recent surveys it is reported that around one third of the food produced, never reaches the consumer. Post harvest losses must be controlled, so as to enhance the income level while men are responsible for constructing storage facilities it is mainly women who maintain and use storage stocks. Once the food has been processed, prepared, and stored, the next vital step is marketing where it has been proved that women play a pivotal role throughout the globe.

Sericulture

Sericulture has emerged as a potential agro-based industry because it is an easy way of afforestation and also gives good returns to the farm women in India silk industry, about 51 per cent of the labour force involved in producing the queen of textile are women. The involvement of women is greater in the activities relating to silkworm rearing, regaling to weaving in garment manufacturing industries. In this particular occupation women are preferred due to dexterity of their fingers in getting the fine filaments from the cocoons and they posses the pertinence to work with hot water steams for ling hours.

Forestry

Women have major role in the forestry sector throughout the developing world. When convinced of the utility and practicability of forestry women can be a strong lobby to persuade other members of the society in the same occupation.

Their involvement in the forestry sector is not limited to collecting fuel and fodder for household but they also form a large fraction of the labour force in forest industries, plantation establishment. Moreover, women are not exclusively subsistence oriented as there agro-forestry preferences include commercial fruits and cash crop trees during agricultural crises, such as drought or flooding, women who are deprived of wage work rely heaving on the gathering and marketing of minor forest products like medicinal plants and herbs, seeds used in condiments industrially important regions etc.

Bio-diversity Conservation

Conservation is a theme which highlights the state of harmony between land and human being. The rural women actively participate in protecting health of the soil through organic recycling and promote crop security through the maintenance of varietal diversity and genetic resistance with their intimate knowledge about various species and their growth characteristics they are particularly keen to maintain biological diversity as they are the ones who use these genetic resources to develop new varieties according to changing needs. The home gardens of women are prefect models of sustainable land use as they provide sustained yields and yet cause' minimal environment degradation under continuous use.

Other Allied Functions

During the last decade mushroom cultivation has become very popular among literate women who can handle the production in a scientific manner women are involved throughout the cultivation process and they posses the skill and patience required to carry on the operation undoubtedly mushroom growing can be an integral part of any development programme involving mainly women to raise their social economic level. The women folk play a significant role in the preservation of excess seasonal fruits and vegetables to be used during lean period. Pickles and jam are often prepared by women for domestic consumption.

Other home based industrial activities of agriculture like cleaning grain storage structures, grading of grains, keeping accounts and taking care of the equipments visualize an active participation of farm women, women manage and organize kitchen gardens in their homes and at their farms near the water sources, for the supply of year round fresh vegetables to meet the daily needs of the family. Apiculture or bee rearing is an activity, which is also gaining a high popularity among the farmwomen.

Problems of Farmwomen

Despite their crucial roles in agricultural development the farmwomen remain as invisible worker suffering severe discrimination. The discrimination is due to gender-biasedness in the society. Though the existing legislation like the equal remunatation Act, the minimum wages Act do not permit any prejudice on the ground of gender, the daily earnings of women labourers are generally less than their male counterpart. The reasons for this disparity are manifold-seasonal nature of the demand for labour unorganized nature of farm labour and poverty and illiteracy coupled with ignorance regarding the laws. Another major problems faced by the farmwomen is the non availability of loans. The financial institutions are hesitant to extend credit to them, as they lack security to offer as collateral. Moreover, these women are unacuare of credit facilities or are unfamiliar with the policies of the institutions and their cumbersome procedures. In spite of women's contribution in agricultural production, they are not given the status of a produces owing to their dependents on the male members since childhood coupled with the inheritance loss and custom, which discriminate against them women are virtually left with nothing to eke out a living on their run. They are in fact the largest group of labourers with little security in case of break up of the family or a divorce. Gender disparity reduces the participation of women not only in employment, but also in the process of economic development. The effect is so severe, that even educated women are oppressed.

There is also a dearth of local women organizations. These organization are capable of making the farmwomen conscious about their rights and privileges as well as regarding improved packages of practices, credit facilities role of government etc.

Government Policies

The concept of women's development has undergone a metamorphic evolution. Initially, it was welfare oriented. In the fifth plan (1974-79) this approach was shifted from welfare to development during the sixth plan (1980-85) the concept of welfare with development services was integrated with multi disciplinary needs of woman viz. health educations etc. In the next plan (1985-90) the government has given a major thrust on economic and social upliftment of women. The eighth plan gives recognition to the role of women in agriculture. It envisages distribution of surplus land to woman-headed household. Emphasis is an the expansion of programme of training in soil conservation, sericulture, poultry etc. besides strengthening the extension service.

Suggestions

Measures would be taken to reduce the element of drudgery among rural women through improved sanitary conditions biogas plants and low cost technologies. The various farmer-training centers which organize training for women take into account the technological needs of women farmers.

Special projects for women, aided by foreign agencies have been taken up in some states to provide training to farmwomen, especially in the erena of skill development in agriculture.

Various programmers like "Financial Assistance to Women Co-operatives". Development of women and children in Rural Areas etc. Spearhead the women's development so as to ensure the national development.

Conclusion

In India there is an increasing trend towards feminization of agriculture. One of the main causes of this phenomenon is the rural-urban migration of men in search of paid employment. To meet the changing socio-economic realities the improvement of technical competence of women in agriculture is a must for an economically and ecologically sustainable agriculture, the involvement of farmwomen is absolutely essential. Keeping in view the past and continued role of women in this sector, efforts must be streamlined towards reduction of drudgery improved productivity and diversified opportunity productive and remunerative employment.

REFERENCES

1. Mallik, R.M. and R.K. Meher, Impact of IRDP on KBK District of Orissa.

2. Meher, Shibalal, "Status of the Natural Resources Environment in Orissa".

3. Eswar Rao Patnaik, "Problems and Prospects of Agricultural Development".

3

Self-Help Groups in Orissa

A Path of Economic Empowerment of Woman (A Case Studies)

*Dr. Bishnu Narayana Sethi**

Micro finance is recognized as a key strategy for addressing issues of poverty allegation and women's empowerment access to financial services and the subsequent transfer to financial resources to poor women enable them to become economic agents to change. Women became self reliant contribute directly to the well-being of their families play a more active role in decision-making and are able to confront systemic gender inequalities.

Access to credit has long been considered a major poverty alleviation strategy in India. Although various credit programmes have been introduced in the country, their impact has proved ineffective. Much of this failure was due to a lack of involvement by the people during any stage of the implementation of the programmes.

In the state of Orissa the Government has been implementing various antipoverty programmes. The major

*Bishnu Narayana Sethi is Sr. Lecturer in Economics, L.N. Dgree College, Kodala I.C.S.S.R (New Delhi) Research Fellow. Member, Board of Studies, Sultan Chand & Sons. Members, Standing Committee Panchayat Samit, Beguniapada. Rover Leader, B.S.G. Bhubaneswar.

objective of these programmes is to generate additional employment, create productive assets and impart technical and entrepreneurial skills and raise the income level of the poor in the rural system. During 2004-05 the government of Orissa has been earmarked a sizeable amount i.e. Rs 40 crore for the rural development rural employment and poverty alleviation programme under State Sector.

Among the various prograrnrnes "Swarna Jayanti Grama Swarozgar Yojana" (SGSY) is an important one. This programme was launched on 1st April 1999 at 75:25 Costs sharing between central and state government.

The main objective of this programmes to being the beneficiaries above the poverty line by providing income generating assets to them through bank credit and government subsidy SHGs are the major component of this scheme.

The Self-Help Group

Self-help groups means small, economically homogeneous affinity group of rural/urban poor, voluntarily formed to save and contribute to a common fund to be lent to its members as per group decision and for working together for social and economic uplift of their families and community. SHGs are (i) A simple but effective method for the poor to help each other (ii) A voluntary group of rural poor who face similar situations and problems (iii) Encourages small savings (thrift) among members (iv) provides a forum for the members to solve their problems collectively (v) Number of members are usually between fifteen and twenty.

In India a number of self-help groups (SHGs) were created in the 1980 for providing credit facilities to the poor, especially women, in both Urban and Rural areas. These SHGs stumbled upon a surprising finding by targeting women; repayment rates came in well over 95 per cent, higher than most traditional banks.

Impressed *b* those repayment rates institution like a National Bank for Agriculture and Rural Development

(NABARD) and Small Industries Development Bank of India (SIDBI) began increasing their lending to SHGs in India. However the lending rates of SHGs, to borrowers were not cheap. For example, SIDBI lent to NGOs at 9 per cent, NGOs were allowed to lend to SHGs rate up to 15 per cent and SHGs in turn were allowed to charge up to 30 per cent and individual borrowers. Although such high interest credit is touted as a vehicle for poverty aviation wherein the poor use the funds to undertake commercial ventures, studies have found that the loans are large used by poor people to met their daily consumption needs.

In Orissa this group is a voluntary one, formed an areas of common interest so that then can think, organise and operate for their development SHGs function on the basis of co-operative principles and provide a forum for members to extent support to each other. It is considered as a means of empowerment SHGs organise very poor people who do not have access to financial system in the organized sector. In groups, normally transparency and accountability are lacking, However, in a group like SHG, they are ensured through collective action of the members this scheme mobilises the poor rural people especially women to form groups for mutual benefits. SHGs play a crucial role in improving the saving s and credit and also in reducing poverty and social inequalities.

The SHGs generally have members not exceeding 20 members and each group select among it members a leader called animator, President and Secretary. The animator called two to three meetings in every month. The group members save regularly Rs. 30 to 100 and more in every month. After complete stabilization in management of its funds the group rotates the Saved money to its needy members as per requirements at a specified low interest rate. Again the SHGs are being linked with the banks through B-MASS at block level and D-MASS (DRDA) at district level for the external credit under the project of rural development. But now the State Bank of India directly provides the financial to the SHGs with low interest rates. The Joint Appraisal Teams

(JATs) consisting of various banks managers, rural development officials, NGOs, project implementation units, BDOS/CDPOS/SEOS/LSEOS of concerned blocks visit the groups and select the beneficiaries as proposed by the groups for providing financial assistance beside focusing on the entrepreneurial development of the beneficiaries and their Villages as a whole, the groups are also undertake the responsibility of developing non-credit services such as literacy, health, sanitation, creating awareness for various awareness programems, environmental issues and related activities.

The group can avail themselves of financial facilities offered by the financial institutions and the government. The individual members can also apply for the credit facilities. However them are certain norms and prescribed procedures for obtaining credit.

Frequently the group should convene meetings of its members and discuss all the issues relating to the groups and a common platform. This provides an opportunity to members to express freely their views exceptions and suggestions for improving the functioning the group. Regularly government agencies and (VDOs) organise training programme for educating and developing skills among members. These programmes enable the members to learn co-operate and work in a group environment. SHGs are required to maintain records as directed by the monitoring agencies.

The Objectives of the Study

The objectives of this study are basically to justify the following:

- That self-help promotion promotes socio-economic development of rural society.
- That Self-help promotion also facilities Socio-economic and intellectual self-reliance of poor women.
- The horizontal and vertical linkages between SHGs are reflected throughp their capital formation capacity

and consequent development of an "Associative economy" to their advantage.

That Self-help Promotion institutions and local NGOs are capable of developing rural activities and economy in the said area.

Methodology

This research is based on field study through both direct and indirect participation with members of SHGs. Questionnaire was distributed among respondents and interview was conducted. Views of local leaders were also sought to analyse women problems perfectly.

Analysis of SHGs MASS-Bank Linkages: (A Case Study in Ganjam District)

Ganjam District of Orissa, the area of study in the context of this article is geographically situated along the East-Coast of the country and in close proximity to the Eastern Ghats. In terms of the Geographical area it is the fifth largest in the state, with a total population of 31,36,937 people (rural population being 25,98,746 and urban population is 3,38.191) which is highest in the state as per the 2001 census estimates (provisional). There are 2816 numbers of revenue villages and 633 numbers of hamlets in the district under 22 blocks (with 17 NACs) and one municipality. As per the 1997 BPL survey report of Panchayat Raj Department. Government of Orissa, there are 548308 families living below the poverty line on the basis of their occupations in the district.

The Orissa state in general and Ganjam District in particular have made pioneering achievements in the evaluation of women led Self-Help Groups (WSHGs). In the year 1998 the Mahila Swayam Sahavak Sangha was experienced for the first time in Orissa State, in the Chatrapur block of the Ganjam district headquarters, which had only 62 WSHGs under its purview. However, within a period of one year, 22 numbers of B-MASS (Block MASS) has been established in all the 22 block headquarters of the

District. By the way, up to December 2001, there are 23 MASS (including 22 B-MASS and one in municipality) under the D-MASS (District MASS) with 4613 numbers of WSHGs.

The present status of WSHs, saving structure, number of defaulters of D-MASS in the Ganjam District is deprived in table below:

Table 3.1: Formation, Saving Status and Loan Repayment of SHGs in the District of Ganjam of Orissa State (Up to August 2004)

Sl.No.		*Description*	*Value*
1.		Total number of MASS under D-MASS	23
2.		SHGs Status	
	(i)	Total enrolment of groups	11159
	(ii)	Total formation of groups	14439
3.		Saving status of SHGs	
	(i)	Total amount of savings (in lakhs)	Rs. 1583.23
	(ii)	Average percentage of groups saving during the last month (July 2004)	71
4.		Saving status of MASS	
	(i)	Enrolment fee collected	Rs. 802710
	(ii)	Total monthly subscription	Rs. 1,15,11,130
	(iii)	Grand total amount	Rs. 1,23,13,840
5.		Irregular Saving Groups (ISGs)	
	(i)	Number of SHGs	4911
	(ii)	Per cent of ISGs	42
6.		Loan repayment of SHGs to MASS	
	(i)	Total dues (principal + Interest)	Rs. 11590 024
	(ii)	Amount received (principal + Interest)	Rs. 7059822
	(iii)	Over due	Rs. 4530202
	(iv)	Per cent of over due	39
	(v)	Per cent of recovery	61

Source: Computed Data.

From the table it can be seen that, there are a total of 14439 numbers of groups formed (upto August 2004) of which 11159 numbers of groups are so far enrolled under D-MASS of Ganjam District. A sum of Rs. 1583.23 lakh at an average of 71 per cent is saved by the WSHGs of the district, amounting of Rs. 1,23,13,840 under HASS (Rs. 802710 is collected towards entrance fee to MASS and Rs. 1,15,11,130 towards monthly subscription). 42 per cent i.e. 4911 numbers of WSHGs are identified as Irregular Savings Groups (ISGs) in the District. The loan repayment status of WSHGs to MASS reveals a sum of Rs. 11590024 as due amount (as principal + interest) out of which Rs. 7059822 is so far rapid (principal) + interest) at a rate of 61 per cent. Similarly, table reveals status of credit linkage and loan repayment of MASS to BANK in the Ganjam District.

Column-3 and Column-1 of Table 3.2 shows total credit status of MASS where as Column-5 and Column-6 shows the credit status of Banks tinder each MASS in the Ganjam District. Column-7 of the table reveals a clear-cut picture of average amount of credit of each MASS separately, along with the figure of D-MASS. Similarly, Column-8 and Column-9 of the table shows the loan repayment status of each MASS in the district as principal amount and interest to the principal amount respectively. Whereas, Column-10 of the table highlights detailed figure of Bank loan along with the amount of loan repayment in Column-11 of the table. Outstanding Bank loan status of each MASS in the District is deprived in Column-12.

Impact of SHGs on Women Empowerment

To find out the percentage distribution of members empowerment regarding the impact of participation of group activity in the district, five groups are considered. As many as five variables are used in each case for assessing social development, economic development and self-confidence aspect of the women of SHGs in the District.

Along with three variables in each case are used for assessing social empowerment aspect and development skill aspects.

The social development values is found to be high in awareness of girl child education (64%) and improvement in

Table 3.2: Credit Linkage and Loan Repayment Status of MASS Bank in Ganjam District

Sl. No.	Name of the MASS	Credit Linkage of MASS-BANK					Loan Repayment of MASS-Bank				
		MASS Structure		of which Bank Link			Repayment				
		Groups	Amounts (in lakhs)	Groups	Amount (in lakhs)	Avg. amount Per Group	Principal (in Rs)	Interest (in Rs)	Bank loan (in lakhs)	Repaid in Lakph)	Out stand-ding Bank Loan
1	2	3	4	5	6	7	8	9	10	11	12
1.	Chatrapur	727	404.77	294	140.34	55677	9150662	1448261	140.34	91.51	48.83
2.	Ganjam	480	146.06	202	65.78	30429	2727165	682546	65.78	27.27	38.51
3.	Khallikote	476	118.58	170	43.62	24912	2131561	422852	43.62	21.32	22.30
4.	K.S. Nagar	465	100.84	175	46.08	21686	3541953	117032	46.08	35.42	10.66
5.	Kukudakhandi	523	113.11	192	48.49	21627	1543785	11.999	48.49	15.44	33.05
6.	Digapahandi	494	118.21	207	41.78	23929	1938120	354930	41.78	19.78	22.40
7.	Chikiti	123	27.52	52	9.39	22374	721557	108729	9.39	7.22	2.17
8.	Patrapur	228	33.40	85	15.16	14649	711700	128525	15.16	7.12	8.04
9.	Bhanganagar	309	37.95	81	11.81	12282	582192	45171	11.81	5.82	5.99
10.	Buguda	220	42.54	52	12.95	19336	477633	23956	12.95	4.78	8.20
11.	J.N. Prasad	551	205.66	205	52.06	37325	1702107	438775	52.06	17.02	35.04
12.	Aska	392	40.07	111	17.30	10222	839398	177568	17.30	8.39	8.91

(Contd...)

Table 3.2: (Contd...)

Sl. No.	Name of the MASS	Credit Linkage of MASS-BANK					Loan Repayment of MASS-Bank				
		MASS Structure of which Bank Link					Repayment		Bank loan (in lakhs)	Repaid in Lakph)	Out standing Bank Loan
		Groups	Amounts (in lakhs)	Groups	Amount (in lakhs)	Avg. amount Per Group	Principal (in Rs)	Interest (in Rs)			
1	2	3	4	5	6	7	8	9	10	11	12
13.	Berhampur	451	96.41	184	68.24	21377	2176000	412058	68.24	21.76	46.48
14.	Beguniapada	423	73.20	100	32.66	17305	625716	70419	32.66	6.26	26.40
15.	Polosara	368	79.69	103	34.55	21655	1110280	31019	34.55	11.10	23.45
16.	Bellaguntha	238	18.77	14	250	7877	51133	18836	2.50	0.51	1.99
17.	Purushottampur	419	67.57	129	33.12	16126	1034009	208406	33.12	10.34	22.78
18.	Sanakhemundi	379	72.58	128	27.28	19150	843693	200667	27.28	8.44	18.44
19.	Hinjilikatu	455	237.42	236	89.78	52180	2846976	572032	89.78	28.47	61.34]
20.	Rangailunda	433	89.80	94	23.18	20739	895249	98991	23.18	8.95	14.23
21.	Dharakot	382	32.98	34	3.82	8634	333815	37126	3.82	3.34	0.48
22.	Sorada	626	193.69	182	71.12	30941	2649555	635964	71.12	26.50	44.62
23.	Seragada	295	52.92	76	12.28	17934	481218	41122	12.28	4.81	7.47
	Total	9457	240.74	3108	903.22		39115477	6388847	903.32	391.15	512.17

personal hygiene, whereas, the value is very low in case of adoption of small family norm (27%) followed by discontinuation of early marriages.

In case of economic development measure. Freedom from the moneylenders has the highest value (96%) followed by control over resources (83%) improvement in banking habits (81%) increase in mobility (69%) whereas in case of increase in self-employment potential the value is low (61%). Out of the three variables examined for assessing Social empowerment, except on awareness of women's right (45%) other two are showing positive sign (i.e. more than 55 per cent in aggregate). Similarly, in the assessment of self-confidence aspect all most all the five items examined shows more than 55 per cent involvement of women in aggregate through SHGs. Whereas, in assessment of development skill with three items, except that of communication skill (52%), other two items are showing more than 55 per cent performance in the Ganjam

Progress Under SHG Bank Linkage Programme in Orissa

So far over 60000 groups have been credit linked thereby providing access to financial service to over 10.71. lakh rural poor families till March 2006 with cumulative Bank disbursement of Rs. 200.00 crore.

In the State during the current years 37000 SHGs have been financed with Bank Loan of Rs. 87.00 crore.

Promotion and Nurturing of SHGs

As regard the promotion and nurturing of SHGs the Women and Child Development Department of the Government of Orissa has been a front runner SHGs promoting agency having stare of 80 per cent SHGs in existence. The other agencies and nearly 100 NGOs that are operative in various district of the State given the large scale of state interventions, state level co-ordination among this organization has become important. The State Government may like to consider evolving a suitable control co-ordination mechanism at the state and district level for a healthy SHGs movement. This would lead to creation of favourable environment for promotion of 1.5 lakh quality SHGs that are required to provide financial inclusions to all the rural poor families in the State.

Promotion of SHG through Farmers Clubs

The idea behind the scheme is to use farmer clubs as extended arms of the bank branches to promote link and monitor SHGs more effectively. Basically it is a scheme for up scaling SHGs promotion by capacity building of the Nodal Bank branches.

Initiatives by NABARD for Banks

(i) Identification of potential and emerging potential districts for promoting and establishing the concept of SHGs.

(ii) Organised divisional SHGs workshops training programme orientation needs, for the benefit of branch managers and staff of different banks. During 2005-06 eight such programmes have been conducted by NABARD.

(iii) Faculty support to different banks for tier in-house programmes on SHGs.

(iv) Regular interaction with Bankers for creation of conductive environment and to overcome operational problems.

(v) SHG award functions is being organized every years to felicitate the best performers of Banks and branches as also NGOs and District administration for their excellent performance under SHGs bank linkage programme.

(vi) Extending exposure to all Block Level Bankers Committee (BLBC) members. The lead District managers and NABARD District Development Managers have been requested to facilitate the exposure visits during the course of conducting BLBC meetings.

(vii) RRB roped in as SHG promoting institutions (SHPIs) and has also been sanctioned grant assistance NABARD would welcome proposal from remaining RRBs to act as SHPIs through grant assistance.

Current Major Problems and Findings

On the basis of the Primary Survey conducted by the investigator among a few units functioning in the State of Orissa.

It is found that SHGs faces problems in different areas. The important problems are briefly stated below:

1. *Ignorance of Members*

Even though the authorities take measures for creating awareness among the group members about the scheme beneficial to them, still majority of the group are unaware of the scheme of assistance offered to them. Now the Government of Orissa offers subsidies and other scheme of assistance up to maximum of Rs. 5 lakh. However many are ignorant.

2. *Inadequate Training Facilities*

The training facilities given to the member of SHGs in the specific areas of product selection, quality of product, production techniques, managerial ability, packing, other technical knowledge etc. are not adequate to compete with that of strong units.

3. *Problems Related with Raw Materials*

Normally each SHGs procures raw materials individuals from the suppliers. They purchase raw materials in smaller quantities and hence they may not be able to enjoy the benefits of large-scale purchase like discount credit facilities etc. Moreover there are no systematic arrangements to collect raw materials in bulk quantities and preserve them properly. There is no linkage with major suppliers of raw materials most of the SHGs are ignorant about the major raw material suppliers and their terms and conditions, all these cause high cost of ratio materials.

4. *Problems of Marketing*

Marketing is an important area of functioning of the SHGs However, they face different problems in the marketing of products produced by them. Following are the major problems reported by SHGs:

(a) Lack of sufficient order.

(b) Lack of linkage with the marketing Agencies.

(c) Lack of adequate sale promotion measures.

(d) Lack of permanent market jot the product of SHG.

(e) Absence of proper brand name.

(f) Poor/Unattractive packing system.

(g) Poor quality of products due to the application of traditional technology, resulting in poor market.

(h) Stiff competition from other major suppliers.

(i) Lack of a well defined and well knit channel of distribution for marketing.

5. *Lack of Stability and Unity Especially Among Women SHGs*

In the case of SHGs, dominated by women, it is found that there is no stability of the units as many married women are not in a position to associate with the group due to the shift of their place of residence. Moreover, there is no unity among women members owing to personal reasons.

6. *Exploitation by Strong Members*

It is found that in the case of a few units strong members try to earn a lion's share of the profit of the groups, by exploiting the ignorant and illiterate members.

7. *Weak Financial Management*

It is also found that in certain units the return from the business is not properly invested further in the unit, and the funds diverted for other personal and domestic purpose like marriage, construction of house etc.

8. Low Return

The return and investment is not attractive in certain groups due to inefficient management, high cost of production, absence of quality consciousness etc.

9. Inadequate Financial Assistance

It is also found that in most of the SHGs, the financial assistance provided to them by the agencies concerned are not adequate to meet their actual requirement. The financial authorities are not giving adequate subsidy to meet even the labour cost requirement.

10. Non-cooperative Attitude of the Financial Institution

They do not consider SHGs seriously while providing finance and other helps.

11. Inadequate and Ill Trained Staff to Meet the Challenges

The attitude of the staff of the rural development department ICDS, Block is not encouraging. They are not well trained to accept the challenges and equip the SHGs, Self-reliant.

12. Inadequate Support from Line Department

For obtained assistance and support the group members have to approach the line officers. However the line officers are not co-operative with the SHGs. This will hamper the very objective of the schemes.

Initiatives Expected from Banks

1. Banks need to identify suitable branches based on potential extent of rural poverty etc. and motivate the staff for active participation in the programme.
2. Planning for SHGs financing may be alone in the Annual credit plans (ACP) every year.
3. Banks are urged to adopt a liberal and flexible approach and devise simplified work procedure/documentations for account opening/credit linking of SHGs.

4. Reporting of performance under SHGs programme in LBRs.

5. Evolving a monitoring mechanism for SHGs financed by the Banks and Submission of data to NABARD regularly.

6. Establish contacts with NGOs/VAs to sort out ground level problems.

7. Delegation of adequate financial power to branch managers for sanctioning of SHGs loans.

Suggestions

1. In Orissa there are plenty of locally available resources. Information about locally available materials and their varied uses should be disseminated to SHGs. Proper encouragement and training should be given to them to make innovative product by using these materials. In order to have a knowledge base about the availability of materials, in Panchayat level surveys can be conducted under the auspices of local authorities.

2. In order to solve the various problems relating to marketing of SHGs the state level organizations should extend the activities through the state instead of limiting its operations a particular area.

3. Various SHGs functioning in a particular Panchayat area can form a Co-operative Society. The society may be encrusted with the task of marketing the products of different SHGs under a common brand name. Further the society can undertake sales promotion activities and procure rare raw materials for the benefits of member SHGs.

4. Non-government Agencies (NGOs) can play a significant role in empowering woman entrepreneurs by providing basic education, motivation training, financial help and so on.

5. All the members in the SHGs may not have the same caliber and expertise. NGOs can identify the inefficient

members of the group and can impart proper training to them in Order to make them competent. For the purpose short term training programmers can be arranged at the panchayat level.

6. Frequent awareness camps can be organized by the Rural Development and Block authorities to create awareness about the different schemes of assistance available to the participants in the SHGs.
7. Arrangement may be made by the financial institutions for providing adequate financial assistance to the SHGs strictly on the basis of their actual performance with out any discrimination of caste, politics etc.
8. To bring uniformity in accounting practices, it is a proposed that a standard accounting practice may be adopted. It will not only bring transparency in transactions but the monitoring will also become easier.
9. To ensure financing of quality groups it is essential to adopt "Rating Norms". In state level review and co-ordination committee on credit delivery innovations (SLRCCDI) it was decided that all the groups must be rated at the time of second linkage.
10. The number of groups is increased and it is therefore necessary to have uniform system of maintenance of data. The group wise date is generally maintained by SHPs through ICDs, NGOs are maintaining.

They are using data at present but different performance. Against this background there is an urgent need to develop uniform system for the purpose.

Conclusion

Various other reviews and evaluations of SHGs programmes suggest that SHGs have provided access to credit to their members helped to prompt savings and yielded moderate economic benefits, reduced that dependence an moneylenders, and resulted in empowerment benefits to women, on the other hand field reports also suggest that contrary to the vision for SHGs development SHGs are generally not composed of mainly the poorest families, there is greater evidence of social empowerment rather than significant and consistent economic impact and financial skill of group members have not developed as planned.

NABARD's corporate mission is to make available MF service to 20 million poorhouse holds or one third of the total poor in the country by 2008. However there is at present a high degree of concentration in the southern states with just two states, Andhra Pradesh and Tamil Nadu accounting for more than 66 per cent of the SHGs receiving loans through bank linkage, with the coverage in Andhra Pradesh being nearly 53 per cent of total SHGS. These states have a history of women enterprise, higher level of literacy and strong cooperative institution SHGs bank linkage has not as yet made in impact in the poverty belt of the northern central and eastern regions.

There are obvious advantage in federation and all Indian states are following this approach, albeit at different speed. In terms of employment generation and enterprise development federations are likely to have a much larger impact than individual SHGs because training and marketing can be organized more rationally. SHGs federation also provides the opportunity for poor people to influence policies and to constitute effective pressure group at the district and state level.

REFERENCES

1. Mallik, R.M. and R.K. Meher. Impact of IRDP and K.B.K. District of Orissa, N.K.C. center for development Studies, Bhubaneswar.

2. Pasayat C. and R.K. Meher, Development Scenario or Orissa District, A Temperal Analysis, Sahabhagi Abhiyan Bhubaneswar, 2004.

3. Pasayat, C., *Rural Development in Orissa; Problems and Potential;* Mohit Publications, New Delhi, 2004.

4. Dr. Sethi, B.N., *Women Development Problems of Discrimination*, Sonali Publication, New Delhi.

5. Dr. Sethi, B.N., *Rural Development Problems and Remedies*, Sonali Publications, New Delhi.

4

Economic Empowerment of Rural Women

A Focus

Balakrishna Padhi (National fellow of U.G.C.)

From the very beginning of Independent India's development planning process, one of the main issue has been that of providing equal status to women. Despite legal and constitutional guarantees, women had lagged behind in almost all sectors. Declining sex ratio and the lower life expectancy of women as the basic indicator of their low status. Currently almost all tile countries of the globe are seriously concern to the problems of gender discrimination, poverty alleviation, terrorism and natural disaster mitigation problems. In the process of development more focus has been given to gender inequality. Gender discrimination arises when there is some unequal treatment on certain privileges to men and women. Today in different sectors gender inequality is all pervasiveness. The agricultural sector is no exception to it. Being India purely an agrarian economy, major portion of its total population depend on agriculture. In this sector both men and women are working together.

Objective of the Study

The main objectives of the study are;

1. To understand the nature and type of torture and problems of women labourer in the agricultural sector.
2. To know whether equal pay far equal work are guaranteed or not.

3. The cause of women labour in agricultural sector.

Methodology Adopted

The data for the study are collected from two sources—Primary and Secondary sources both interview method and observation method has been designed to make the study more intensive. For the purpose of the study a suitable questionnaire is designed. The questionnaire is shaped to know the socio-economic conditions of the women labourer particularly in agricultural sector. All the primary data is collected through personal interviews. For these fifty house holds as a samples are taken to choose women workers who are actively engaged rural agricultural sectors. Purposively. Village Tarasingi has been selected for the study. Majority of the inhabitants of the village are engaged as agricultural labourers due to non-availability of alternative source of employment. In agricultural sector, there is glaring disparities in daily wage, nature of work hours etc.

Further it is seen that though women are actively engaged in agricultural sector, but their participation rate are not equal with their male counterpart. This is depicted in Table 4.1.

Table 4.1: Participation Ratio of Female in Agricultural Sector

Census	*T/R/U*	*Female*	*Male*	*Persons*
1981	Total	19.7	52.6	36.7
	Rural	23.1	53.8	38.8
	Urban	8.3	49.1	30.0
1991	Total	22.3	51.6	37.5
	Rural	26.8	52.6	40.1
	Urban	9.2	48.9	301.2
2001	Total	25.7	519	39.3
	Rural	31.0	52.4	42.0
	Urban	11.6	50.9	32.2

Sources: Census of India, Government of India.

Table 4.2

Household	*Wage rate*		*Illiteratei/Literate*		*Sector*			
					Agr.		*Non.Agr.*	
	M	*F*	*M*	*F*	*M*	*F*	*M*	*F*
1	50	30	Literate	Illiterate	-	Agr.	Non-Agr.	
2	50	30	Literate	Literate	-	Agr.	Non-Agr.	-
3	50	30	Literate	Illiterate	Agr.	Agr.	-	-
4	50	30	Literate	Illiterate	-	Agr.	Non-Agr.	-
5	50	30	Literate	Illiterate	-	Agr.	Non-Agr.	-
6	50	30	Literate	Literate	Agr.	Agr.	Non-Agr.	-
7	50	30	Literate	Illiterate	-	Agr.	Non-Agr.	-
8	50	30	Literate	Illiterate	-	Agr.	Non-Agr.	Non-Agr.
9	50	30	Literate	Illiterate	Agr.	Agr.	-	-
10	50	30	Literate	Illiterate	-	Agr.	Non-Agr..	-
11	50	30	Literate	Literate	Agr.	Agr.	-	-
12	50	30	Literate	Illiterate	-	Agr.	Non-Agr.	-
13	50	30	Literate	Illiterate	-	Agr.	Non-Agr.	-
14	50	30	Literate	Illiterate	-	Agr.	Non-Agr.	-
15	50	30	Literate	Illiterate	-	Agr.	Non-Agr.	-
16	50	30	Literate	Illiterate	Agr.	Agr.	-	-
17	50	30	Literate	Illiterate	Agr.	-	Non-Agr.	-

Table 4.2: (Contd...)

Household	Wage rate		Illiteratei/Literate		Sector			
					Agr.		Non. Agr.	
	M	F	M	F	11	F	M	F
18	50	30	Literate	Illiterate	Agr.	Agr.	-	-
19	50	30	Literate	Literate	-	Agr.	Non-Agr.	-
20	50	30	Literate	Illiterate	-	Agr.	Non-Agr.	-
21	i0	30	Illiterate	Literate	-	Agr.	Non-Agr.	-
22	0	30	Literate	Illiterate	-	Agr.	Non-Agr.	-
23	50	30	Literate	Illiterate	-	Agr.	Non-Agr.	-
24	50	30	Illiterate	Illiterate	Agr.	Agr.	-	-
25	50	30	Literate	Illiterate	-	Agr.	Non-Agr.	-
26	50	30	Literate	Illiterate	-	Agr.	Non-Agr.	-
27	50	30	Literate	Literate	-	Agr.	Non-Aer,	-
28	50	30	Literate	Illiterate	Agr.	Agr.	-	-
29	50	30	Literate	Literate	-	Agr.	Non-Agr.	-
30	50	30	Literate	Illiterate	-	Agr.	Non-Agr.	-
31	50	30	Literate	Illiterate	-	Agr.	Non-Agr.	-
32	50	30	Literate	Illiterate	Agr.	Agr.	-	-
33	50	30	Literate	Illiterate	Agr.	Agr.	-	-
34	50	30	Illiterate	Illiterate	-	Agr.	Non-Agr.	-

(Contd...)

Table 4.2: (Contd...)

Household	*Wage rate*		*Illiteratei/Literate*		*Sector*			
					Agr.		*Non.Agr.*	
	M	*F*	*M*	*F*	*11*	*F*	*M*	*F*
35	50	30	Illiterate	Illiterate	-	Agr.	Non-Agr.	-
36	50	30	Literate	Illiterate	-	Agr.	Non-Agr.	-
37	50	30	Literate	Literate	-	Agr.	Non-Agr.	-
38	50	30	Literate	Illiterate	Agr.	Agr.	-	-
39	50	30	Literate	Illiterate	-	Agr.	Non-Agr.	-
40	50	30	Literate	Illiterate	Agr.	Agr.	Non-Agr.	-
41	50	30	Literate	Illiterate	-	Agr.	–	-
42	50	30	Literate	Literate	-	Agr.	Non-Agr.	-
43	50	30	Literate	Illiterate	-	Agr.	Non-Agr.	-
44	50	30	Literate	Illiterate	Agr.	Agr.		-
45	50	30	Literate	Illiterate	Agr.	Agr.	Non-Agr.	-
46	50	30	Literate	Literate	Agr.	Agr.	-	-
47	50	30	Illiterate	Illiterate	-	Agr.	Non-Agr.	-
48	50	30	Literate	Illiterate	-	Agr.	Non-Agr.	-
49	50	30	Literate	Literate	-	Agr.	Non-Agr.	-
50	50	30	Literate	Illiterate	Agr.	Agr.	Non-Agr.	-
			Illi. Total (M) 6 Nos	Illi. Total (F) 39 No	17	48	33	02

Source: Field study (Primary Data Collection).

The table exhibited that there has been a slight increase in the female work participation rate from 19.7 per cent in 1981 to 25.7 per cent in 2001 this is still much lower than the male work participation rate in both rural and urban areas.

In the informal or unorganized sector women constitute 90 per cent of the total workers. (80% are engaged in agricultural and allied sector and 10 per cent in other sectors.) Moreover unskilled workers constitute 90 per cent of rural and 70 per cent of urban women workers. Such women have to perform domestic duties and also supplement, the family income; since they are unskilled they do not have any principal occupation. They are subjected to economic exploitation with low and discriminatory wages.

Major Findings of the Study

1. There is glaring disparity between male and female worker relating to daily wages. While a male worker get 50 rupees, an women labour receives only 30 rupees as daily wages for the same labour.
2. The participation ratio of women labourers are not equal with male labourers which exhibits in Table 4.1.
3. Low literacy rate among the rural women labour compel low bargaining of wage rate, even though they contribute the same physical labour.
4. The nature of work is more pain taking than their male counterpart example—while sampling Paddy they have to bend their back bone for uncertainty period of time.
5. In the agricultural sector, the hours of working is more than the organized sector, for extra work there is no extra payment.
6. Since agricultural sector is seasonal by nature more than 5 to 6 months the women labourers become unemployed due to their illiteracy and unskilled nature, they are unable to divert to any other alternative occupations,

besides they lack social mobility there is social criticisms of a women if she goes to far off places.

7. Since, women receives very low wages she does not take care her health properly by taking superior vitaminized foods. Out of the little income she supports the wanting of her children.
8. It is interviewed that women agricultural labour performs double duties such as labour in agricultural field and busy in domestic duties.
9. From the survey further it is informed that when the crops are harvested, the disposal of the crops is enjoyed by the male while the women plays zero role.
10. Out of fifty samples six women have informed that their hard earnest 30 rupees daily wage is misutilised by their respective drunkard husbands. In urgent cases there is no single penny with them even to buy a minor capsule.

Empowerment of Women

Empowerment means enhancing the capacity and efficiency of an individual in every sphere. Thus empowerment is a multidimensional and refers to the expansion of freedom of choice and action in social economic as well as political spheres. It shape one's life and increases his capability and activities in all most all decision-making and control over resources. Due to widespread gender inequality and injustice in the household as well as in society. Empowerment or freedom of women is often severely curtailed. Thus for empowerment of women require to uplift the condition of some socio-economic factors. Such as health education, environment employment at the individual level and to initiate, organize or control over all their income earning activities at the collective level empowerment of women in India is still in negligible position. Hence, this is the need of the hour, we should encourage and improve the social status of women in both domestic and social grounds.

India is an agricultural country. The vast majority of the people in India live in rural areas and are engaged in agricultural earning. They get subsistence wage for their work. Half of the rural population involves women folk. However, they are unable to act independently in economic activities and decision-making among their families and societies as well. Hence the rural women have acquired a secondary status in social life. The women workers engaged in agricultural field, generally their role in employment generation, work productivity. Income oriented activities are largely influenced by many socio-economic and cultural constraints. On account of these reasons there exists gender gap in the society. To enhance the socio-economic conditions of rural women. Especially, agricultural women labourers more attention has to be given to provide universalization of primary education and proper management and expansion of adult education. Improve health and civic conditions of rural women. Especially, those works in agricultural and allied sectors. The main reasons which hampers the women empowerment are given below:

Education

The greatest hindrance to the progress of India and eradication of many social evils of her people is illiteracy of the masses. Since India is an agricultural land. Majority of women in rural area occupied agriculture as their main livelihood. Excessive illiteracy among rural women has given them a primary role in homemaking and in household activities, which is unpaid and unrecognized. In India, most of the women living in rural areas are illiterate and falls in vicious circle of poverty and deprivation. The proportion of women is high among the poor and illiterate persons. Lack of education among women in rural areas hampers economic development and the rural women lying inferior and inactive in every sphere as compared to their male counterpart. Due to illiterate and ignorance among rural agricultural women labourer they are subjected to gender inequality in several ways. Such as wage discrimination hours of work and nature of work etc. On account of discrimination against women labourers, they forced to receive lower wage and they can be exploited for longer hours for meager wages and can even be used in hazardous and unhygienic work environment. Hence, literacy for poor women is a tool for empowerment in a wider struggle against inequality and injustice.

Health and Nutrition

Health plays crucial role in improving the participation of agricultural women labourers in various activities due to lack of health facilities, Women occupy the lowest priority in poor or lower middle class families. Which leads to inferiority among the women through the process of socialization. Except health, the minimum calorie in take of superior foods is very low, in case of women as compared to male members of the families. So, that the health condition of women workers are neglected and they come down with many contagious diseases.

Poverty

The status of rural women in India is very much adversely affected due to poverty in poor families little importance is given to female members. Poverty also encourages a psychological hatred towards female members as she is considered as inferior member of the family. Thus, poverty leads to general economic backwardness of women in a male dominated society and this ultimately accounts for the deprivation of women from enjoying equal rights and opportunities with men in poor agricultural families the man-women relationship is worsened.

Superstition

In India, every activity of life is associated with some sort of superstitions which is mostly prevalent among rural illiterate women folk so long as men do not know everything and so long as there is a mystery around us superstition will exist. In backward countries like India, wide spread illiteracy and less accessible of rural women into education forced them to believe in superstition. The age-old custom's and traditions which are still prevalent in our country are untouchability, purdah system etc. Which are stands on the way of socio-economic development and productivity of rural agricultural women to a great extent. Owing to this there remains a gender gap in all spheres. Hence, empowerment of women has remained a distant goal.

Violence Against Women

The family is very sacred institution in India and women occupy a very important place in the family. The existence of joint family system in India. Apart from wife and husband their old parents, young and minor children, other unemployed youths live together, in such a joint family system the burden of managing the house. Mostly falls upon the women. In poor or middle class families, although women work hard, they have not got sufficient food and they have to be left contented after all members of the house have finished their meals. Which may tells upon the health of the women—in a male dominance society women are faced with many domestic and social violence. Sometimes the women are tortured by her drunkard husband and other family members on the basis of dowry. Similarly in agricultural fields, women workers get less wage as compared to male even if they doing hard labour and in sometimes they assaulted by male workers. On account of these violence against women. Women would not take part actively in education, Employment, income generation and developmental and decision making etc.

In the aforesaid context, it is pertinent to suggest the following options to empower the rural women.

Suggestions

(i) Top priority should be given to women education. Women should be encouraged to take up vocational education in rural areas. The Government should give top priority for registering women education.

(ii) Attempt should be made to increase the income generating activities and independence of women in decision-making. So that the status of women would be increased.

(iii) Appropriate laws should be passed to fight against social evils and practices. Such as dowry, insult and harassment of women, rape, torture, humiliation and discrimination against women and other unhealthy social customs and prejudices.

(iv) The women should develop a consciousness of common interest. In order to protect their rights and personalities and enhance their social prestige. It can be possible only when women help. Each other and united themselves through various organizations and associations.

(v) Adequate protection should be given to women employees against the evil practices of male employees. Especially in agricultural fields.

(vi) Media should play crucial role both in creating awareness about women problems and difficulties and fighting injustices and inequalities against them.

(vii) The voluntary women organizations and NGO's should take active role and come forward to fight against injustice and by creating social awareness among them.

(viii) For improvement of health and civic conditions of rural women. The Government should take leading role in forming public health centers, Hospital, Maternity care centers etc. in village levels.

(ix) The Government should take various rural development works to eradicate poverty and unemployment among women.

REFERENCES

1. Dr. Paul Deepika Yojana, Jan., 2005, Gender and Planning.
2. Census Report, Government of India, 2001.

5

A Focus on Women Empowerment

Dr. Rajendra Sahu
Sr. Journalist, BBSR

Women's empowerment is a global issue, and discussion on women's rights are at the forefront of many formal and informal campaigns worldwide. Empowerment and a word widely used, but seldom defined. Empowerment is an active, multi-dimensional process which enables women to realize their full identity and powers in all spheres of life. Power and not a commodity to be translated, for can it be given away as aims. Power has to be acquired and once acquired, it needs to be exercised, sustained and preserved.

Empowerment and a process and is not, therefore, somethings that can be given to people. The process of empowerment is both individual and collective, since it is through involvement in groups that people most often begin to develop their awareness and the ability to organize to take action and bring about change. Women's empowerment can be viewed as a continuum of several interrelated and mutually reinforcing components. Since empowerment is a necessary part of any intervention to enhance women's income, it is essential to understand some of the critical tenets of empowerment.

According to Jakarta Declaration, 1994, "Women represent fifty per cent of population, makeup thirty per cent of the official labour force, perform sixty per cent of all working hours, receive ten per cent of the world income and own even less than one per cent of the world property." This is the lawful economic profile of women in the world. This is also true of Indian women, and very much true of rural women.

Rural women in our country suffer from being both economically and socially 'invisible'. Economic invisibility stems from the perception that women are not relevant to the wage and market economy social invisibility is a result of the general status of second class citizens, usually accorded to women. The growing realization that rural women are not in articulate, illiterate and ignorant objects of welfare, but are in fact productive, hard working adults, who have coped with the battle for survival from very young age takes their participation in the development process increasingly necessary and imperative.

Women are considered as a weaker sex. They were given a subordinate status in the Hindu Society. "She is protected by the father in her childhood, by the husband in her adulthood and by the son in her old age." The male dominated paternal system allows her to survive as secondary member of the family and lower citizens of society.

The majority of Indian women resides in rural areas and urban slums and the majority of women workers engaged in subsistence agriculture and the informal sector with little or no regulation, legislative protection and trade union support.

The concept of women's empowerment, throughout the world, has its roots in women's movement. It is since the mid-1980's that this term became popular in the field of development, especially in the reference to women. In India, it is the Sixth five year plan (1980-85) which can be taken as a landmark for the cause of women. It is her that the concept of women and development was introduced for the first time. It was realized that no more piecemeal strategies but an integrated approach would deliver the desired goods.

Women's empowerment can be viewed as a continuum of several interrelated and mutually reinforcing components:

- Awareness building about women's situations, discrimination and rights and opportunities as a step towards gender equality, collective awareness building provides a sense of group identity and the power of working as a group.
- Capacity building and skills development; especially the ability to plan, make decisions, organize, manage and carryout activities, to deal with people and institutions in the world around them.
- Participation and greater control and decision-making power in the home, community and social.
- Action to bring about greater equality between men and women.

Indian development planning has always aimed at removing inequalities in the process of development to ensure that the fruits of development are an equal privilege of all. In recent years it has become increasingly evident that women are lagging behind a great deal both in availing of the benefits of development and as participants in the process of development due to several socio-economic cultural-political impediments. This has become a cause for concern since women number several millions and constitute nearly half of our population.

In the early years of planning the concern of gender took a welfarism perspective which manifesto. Itself in the farm of grants, waivers, subsidies and free ships for girls and women in a few relevant programmes. But these concessions did not elicit the required level of participation. In the later half of the 1970's focus shifted from merely welfare to development and greater emphasis on integration of women into the mainstream of social and economic development. In due course many social and economic, programmes like non-formal Education for girls, Integrated

Rural Development Programme were evolved exclusively for women or with percentage set aside solely for them. The benefits derived from these programme had to be sustained and this was posing a challenge. Studies have shown that 'practical gender gains' in improved livelihood, education, nutrition and sanitation are not sustained and easily reversed if the 'strategic need' to give women a voice in the decisions that so directly affect their lives, is not adequately taken care of. The strategy in the 1990's has shifted to empowerment of women and giving them a voice.

It is in this context of empowerment and given the vulnerability and powerlessness of the individual women in the existing socio-economic set up that 'group' strategies acquire great relevance. The formation of small informal functional, groups of women would give them 'visibility' and create micro level power pockets. Further, group would initiate a learning process through sharing of ideas, skills and interactive capacity and in course of time women would learn to articulate their needs resulting in more appropriate participatory and grassroots level plans for them. Some social barriers would also broken in the process. Many groups in recent years have started cutting across barriers of religion and caste and working together harmoniously for economic betterment.

Poverty hits women the hardest, as they balance means and ends at the household level and many a time skip a meal to let the rest off the household avail of the little that is available. These women and subjected to economic and social discrimination, and credit is not easily available to them. Millions of our women live in poverty and their social empowerment would have little relevance without first empowering them on the economic front. The World Bank studies have shown that enhancement of women's earnings would have a more profound effect on the welfare of the family as a whole since increase in women's income result more directly into better health and nutrition for children. Thus grouping women for economic empowerment is of great importance.

The programme for Development of Women and Children in Rural Areas (DWCRA), launched in 1982-83 inaugurated an era for systematically oganising women in groups for enhance their earnings on a self-sustaining basis and increasing their access to and utilization of services like health, child care and adult education, among others. The programme called for formation groups of 10-15 women who would collectively engage in an activity. A revolving fund of Rs. 15000 was made available to early group for credit and administrative needs. Supplementing of staff by inclusion of an additional 'Gram Sevaika' and appointment of a lady officer to the post of Assistant Project Officer to oversee implementation to the programme were called for. Subsequently with a view to fortifying the programme further and increasing awareness a Community Based Convergent Services (CBCS) component and Information, Education and Communication (IEC) component mere included. Upto early 1996, over 1-3 lakh groups covering 2.2 million women were formed. Almost all the districts in the country are presently covered under this programme.

Formation of Thrift and Credit groups of women for self-help and economic self reliance has also been encouraged by the government. A Rashtriya Mahila Kosh (RMK) was set in 1993 for extending credit with low transaction costs to poor and needy women and women's groups through Non-Government Organisations (NGO's).

The Indira Mahila Yojana (IMY) launched in 1995 aims at co-ordianting and integrating sectoral programmes relevant to women like health, education, water, sanitation, housing, and other local, block and district levels and increasing their awareness and income through group activities and participation with the aim of empowering women. Now Mission-Shakthi programme has launched in various states.

In the Centre Government is trying to empower women economically, but social backwardness of women, defective Government' system cannot fulfil all the objects in full.

6

Role of DIC in the Economic Upliftment of Women under PMRY Scheme: *A Study*

*Dr. Sudhansu Sekhar Nayak**
R.L. Panigrahy

Introduction

Economic empowerment of women is an indicator of human development and social progress. So, it is highly essential that women should take active part in the development of the nation. Educational, Economic, Social and cultural empowerment of women would become an important factor. In recent year the themes of "Gender Justice" and "women empowerment" have received adequate attention of the Government of developed as well as developing nations. The debate on gender development and population planning has received much attention only after center national conference on women at Bejing in 1995 and social summit conference held at Copenhagen in 1995. According to United Nations statistics:

1. constitute half of the world's population,
2. women perform 57 per cent of the world's working house,

*Dr. Nayak, Lecturer in Commerce, Ramanarayan College, Dura-10 Ganjam (Orissa).

3. they earn 10 per cent of world's income,
4. women are 2/3rd of the world's illiterates.
5. The own less than 1 per cent of world's property.

70 per cent of them are literate. The health status of majority of women is not sound and they are also not sufficiently involved in decision-making process. Eradication of illiteracy among women is an essential ingredient for the development of the country. Despite various measures taken, the status of women continues to remain backward. It is the policy of the Government, to bring them into the mainstream.

Scope and Objectives

The District Industries Centre (DIC) taking a important role in establishing of small scale industries (SSI) in the state of Orissa. The present study aims to highlight the role played by the DIC in Ganjam district of Orissa in establishing SSI units under Prime Minister's Rojagar Yojana (PMRY) by the women beneficiaries. For the purpose of the study, the Ganjam district is taken as the sample district. The period of the study is limited to four years i.e., 2001-01 to 2003-04 and only secondary datas are taken into consideration. The relevant the secondary data are collected from the annual action plan and official records of DIC in Ganjam district. So, all limitations of the secondary data are bound in this study.

Analysis

The PMRY, a Central Plan Scheme, launched on 2nd October 1993 was originally targeted to provide self-employment opportunities to educated unemployed youths in urban areas only. From 1994-95, the scheme has been extended to rural areas only youths in the age group of 18 to 35 years with minimum educational qualification of Class VIII pass and having annual family income of Rs. 40,000 or less are eligible to avail loan assistance upto Rs. 200 lakh under the scheme. The analysis of the study is divided into three parts:

1. Progress of women beneficiaries under PMRY scheme in Ganjam district.
2. Defaulter position of women beneficiaries under PMRY scheme in Ganjam district.
3. Sickness position of women beneficiaries under PMRY scheme in Ganjam district.

1. Progress of Women Beneficiaries under PMRY Scheme

Progress of women beneficiaries under PMRY scheme in Ganjam district from the period 200-01 to 2003-04 are explained in the Table 6.1.

Table 6.1 shows that, in the PMRY scheme for the years 2000-01 to 2003-04, 695 number of cases of women beneficiaries were recommended to bank for sanction of loan against the numbers of applications received by DIC which was 1,223. Out of this, 242 numbers of cases have been sanctioned with an amount of Rs. 172.66 lakh of this, 167 number of cases have been reported to be disbursed with an amount of Rs. 87.62 lakh grounding 156 number of units and creating an employment of 312 during last 4 years in the Ganjam district.

2. Defaulter Position of Women Beneficiaries under PMRY Scheme

Defaulter position of women beneficiaries under PMRY scheme in Ganjam district from the period 2000-01 to 2003-04 are analysed in the table 6.2.

Table 6.2 shows that, during these four year, 2007 number of women beneficiaries were defaulter in repayment of bank loan as against 167 number of disbursed class which accounts for only 4.2 per cent under PMRY scheme in Ganjam district. From the study, it is clear that the women beneficiaries are very prompt in payment of bank loan in comparison to men beneficiaries under PMRY scheme in Ganjam district during these period of study.

Table 6.1: Progress of Women Beneficiaries under PMRY Scheme in Ganjam District (Rs. in lakh)

Year	Application Received by DIC No.	Recommended to Bank No.	Sanction		Disbursement		Units Grounded No.	Employment No.
			No.	Amount	No.	Amount		
2000-01	495	240	86	63.64	51	24.30	48	96
2001-02	217	124	40	28.90	30	18.50	27	54
2002-03	249	160	55	36.60	51	21.30	39	78
2003-04	262	171	61	43.52	45	23.52	42	84
Total	**1,223**	**695**	**242**	**172.66**	**167**	**87.62**	**156**	**312**

Source: Annual Action Plan, PMRY, 2003-04, DIC, Ganjam.

Table 6.2: Defaulter Position of Women Beneficiaries under PMRY Scheme in Ganjam District

Year	*Sanction No.*	*Disbursement No.*	*Defaulter No.*	*% of Defaulter*
2000-01	86	51	03	5.8
2001-02	40	30	02	6.6
2002-03	55	41	01	2.4
2003-04	61	45	01	2.2
Total	**242**	**167**	**07**	**4.2**

Source: Annual Action Plan, PMRY, 2003-04, DIC, Ganjam.

3. *Sickness position of Women beneficiaries under PMRY Scheme*

Sickness position of women beneficiaries under PMRY scheme in Ganjam district during the period 2000-01 to 2003-04 are discussed in the table 6.3.

Table 6.3: Sickness Position of Women Beneficiaries under PMRY Scheme in Ganjam District

Year	*Units Established No.*	*Sick units No.*	*% of Sickness*
2000-01	48	09	18.7
2001-02	27	05	18.5
2002-03	39	03	7.6
2003-04	42	02	4.7
Total	**156**	**19**	**12.17**

Source: Annual Action Plan, PMRY, 2003-04, DIC, Ganjam.

Table 6.3 reveals that, out of 156 number of SSI units established by the women beneficiaries under PMRY scheme in the district, 19 number of SSI units were bound sick and the percentage of sickness is only 12.17 per cent. From the study, it is clear that the lessen number of SSI units established by the women beneficiaries became sick in comparison to men beneficiaries under PMRY scheme in Ganjam district during these period of study.

Suggestions

Various measures have been suggested for the empowerment of women's education and development. These measures are:

1. The media can play a great role both in creating awareness about women's problems and fighting injustice against them.
2. Progressive laws should be passed to fight against civil practices like dowry, discrimination against women, insult or harassment of women and other unhealthy social customs and traditions.
3. Top priority should be given to the education of women. Effective enforcement of compulsory or vocational education and creation of social climate among the village community to enroll all girls of school going age.
4. Initiating action and participating in educative propaganda to breakdown traditional prejudices against good's education.
5. The central and state governments should join hands and seek the cooperation of different voluntary organizations for the expansion of girls education in every nook and corner of the country.

REFERENCES

1. Lekhi, R.K. The Economics of Development and Planning, Kalyane Publishers, New Delhi, 2005.
2. Dutta, Rudra & Sundaram, K.P.M., Indian Economy, S. Chand and Sons, New Delhi, 2006.
3. Das, K.K. Current Problems in Indian Education, Scientific Book Depot., Orissa, Cuttack, 1984.
4. Nanda, S.K. Indian Education and its Problems Today, Kalyani Publishers, New Delhi, 1977.

5. Dhengara, I.C., Indian Economy, Kalyani Publishers, New Delhi, 2006.

6. Annual Action Plan, PMRY, DIC, Ganjam, 2003-04.

7. Economic Survey Directorate of Economics and Statistics, Orissa, Bhubaneswar, 2005-06. & 2006-07.

8. Districts at a Glance, Government of Orissa, Bhubaneswar, 2007.

9. Statistical Abstracts, Government of Orissa, Bhubaneswar, 2005.

7

Women Empowerment in India: *An Introduction*

Dr. Dasarathi Bhutan

A human being is born free. In other words every individual has the right to a life of freedom. Women are neither etherial nor dolls nor bundles of passions and nerves. They are as much human beings as men are and they are filled with the same urge for freedom. But in the name of social customs and traditions the woman of this country is bound by the claims of slavery forged by men and her freedom is being negated.

Manu, the ancient law given of Indian society ordained that, a woman is not entitled to freedom and independence and that she shall be protected by her father in childhood, by her husband in her youth and by her male children in old age. Hence the concept that women are inferior to men was universally accepted by people in the ancient period and the doors to self development were closed to them. The widow has to observe very hard rules in respect of her food, dress and habits. The peasant labour women do not get wages equal to these of men. The common women become victims to the cruelty of their husbands. They are even haunted by punishment here on earth and elsewhere in imaging hell after their death for breach of duty towards their male counter-parts. The old institutions like caste, patriarchal family, religions moves and dominant social value systems still region supreme with considerable rigour. All these institutions and ideologies are surcharged with the spirit of male dominance. The dowry system, the bride burning. The exploitation of the sex symbol images of women in advertising are the proof of gross injustice against women.

Atrocities and discrimination are the two major problems, which the Indian women face in the present day society. The traditional mentalities of India assume that the place of women is mainly concentrated to the household activities like kitchen work and upbringing of the children. They have been considered as the sex object and inferior to the man in different spheres of knowledge. The 'sati pratha', 'pardah system', 'child marriage' 'dowry system' etc. have been some form of atrocities and discriminatory attitudes against the women.

At the time of British rule, Mahatma Gandhi, knowing the potential of women, advocated the cause of womens' emancipation and influenced them to participate in the freedom struggle of India. Jawaharlal Nehru also supported women's cause and declared that, in order to awaken the people it is the women who have to be awakened, when women are on the move, the village moves, the house hold moves and the country moves.

Even after fifty seven years of Indian independence, women are still one of the most powerless and marginalized sections of Indian society. The 2001 census shows that the sex ratio for India is 933, which is lowest in the world, percentage of female literacy is 54.16 against male literacy of 75.85 per cent. In India, women's representation in parliament and in the state assembles has never beyond 8 and 10 per cent respectively. Most of the working women remain outside the organized sector. A more 2.3 per cent women are administrators and managers, 20.5 per cent professional and the technical workers all of whom collectively earn 25 per cent of the shared income. Violence against women is an the rise.

After the Independence, the crowning achievement of modern Indian history is the recognition and granting of equal status to women through the constitution of free sovereign India. The Constitution has proclaimed the equality of man and woman in all domains of life. The constitution of India in its Article 15 says that the state shall not discriminate against any citizen, on ground only of religion, sex, place or any of them.

Article 16 further says about the equality of opportunity in matters of public employment, the state can make no discrimination on the grounds of religion, race, caste, sex descents or place of birth. Article 23 of the Indian Constitution prohibits traffic in human beings. The constitution in which embodies the directive principles of state policy directs the state under article 39 that, the citizens, men and women equally, have right to an adequate means of livelihood.

The Indian Government has passed various legislations to safeguard constitutional rights to women. The 73rd and 74th Constitution Amendment Act of 1993 provides for one-third reservation of seats in the local bodies of panchayats and municipalities for women. The 84th Constitutional Amendment Act, 1998 which will provide 33 per cent seats in Parliament and State legislatures is in the pipeline. Other legislative measures include, the Hindu Marriage Act, (1955), the Hindu Succession Act, 1956, Dowry Prohibition Act, 1961, Medical Termination of Pregnancy Act, 1971, Equal Remuneration Act 1976, Child Marriage Restraint Act, 1976, Immoral Trafficking Prevention Act 1986 and finally Pre-Natal Diagnostic Technique (Regulation and Prevention of Measure) act 1994 etc. Apart from these, various welfare measures have been taken up by the government from time to time to empower to the women. They are, the support to Training for Employment Programme 1987, Mahila Samriddi Yojana 1993, The Rashtriya Mahila Kosh (1992-93), Indira Mahila Yojana 1995, DWACRA plan 1997 and Balika Samriddhi Yojana 1997 on 12th July 2001, the Mahila

Samriddhi Yojana and Indira Mahila Yojana have been merged into the integrated self-help group programme i.e. Swayan Siddha.

The Government of India established a Central Social Welfare Board in 1953 with a nation-wide programme for grants-in-aid for women-children and under privileged group. A separate department of women and child development was set up at the centre in 1985 to give a district identity and provide a nodal point on matters relating to Women's development. National Commission on women was created by on Act of Parliament in 1992. Besides these India has also ratified various international conventions and human rights instruments committing equal rights of women. Key among them is the fortification of the Convention of Elimination of all Forms of Discrimination Against Women (CEDAW) in 1993.

It is now high time to change our social outlooks towards women. Their understanding, cooperation and effective participation are essential for bringing about the desirable social changes. To quote Smt. Indira Gandhi, "if women are neglected, humanity is deprived of half of its energy and creativity". Therefore for the development of community and nation, for reducing the male dominance and in order to minimize the dissemination against women, they should be brought into the mainstream of social-economic field of the country.

Swami Vivekananda, the famous Indian monk had declared that education is the only panacea for the upliftment of the nation. But we are having an outmoded system of education. This educational system was evolved by the British with a calculated objective of producing men and women suitable for white collar jobs in their administrative hierarchy. But now our thinking is that, our educational should be programmed to train men and women not only who seek employment but also those who would created employment. Therefore the education should be develop such skill and attitude for potential employment. Women should be given proper vocational education and general education, consistent with the need of the society. By proper employment, the women will be able to enhance their family income, their standard of living and can thereby able to raise their social positions and respectability.

Economic and Political Empowerment

Economic and political empowerment of women is the determining factor for development and participate in many spheres of life. As long as "women in India", declared Mahatma Gandhi in 1925, "do not take part in public life there can be no salvation of the country." He further added, "As long women do not come to public life and purify it... we are not likely to attain Swaraj." Even if we did, he added, "I would have no use for that kind of Swaraj to which such women have not made their full contribution."

We are yet to realize the vision of Mahatma Gandhi. It is said that "Doors to economic and political opportunities for women have been opening more slowly and reluctantly" and "the continuing exclusion of women from many economic and political opportunities is a continuing indictment of modern progress." Today women are in the forefront to put an end to this sad chapter of human history.

Women getting the right to vote in America has been considered as more important than manufacture of atom bomb, establishment of United Nations and many other great scientific discoveries. If such is the importance of women getting right to vote then their full participation in political and economic fields will become the most far reaching and important event in the history of mankind.

Substantive portion of women's empowerment rests on the economic independence of women. Woman have least access to credit, property, and economic and productive resources. We have seen how the activities of ordinary women in many parts of the country led to their economic empowerment. The anti-arack movement of Nellore district started by a neo-literate lady Rosamma led to formation of thousands of credit co-operatives and self-help groups which released women from indebtedness and subsequently generated employment for them. These credit cooperatives started by women have been replaced in many other parts of Andhra Pradesh and many other states of India. SEWA Bank in Gujarat, Bhramarambha Mahila Cooperative Bank in Andhra Pradesh and many other such women's banks are shining examples of women's active involvement in promoting their economic empowerment. Andhra Pradesh has also taken the first step in establishing separate industrial estate for women. Started by the Association of Lady Entrepreneurs of Andhra Pradesh it has become a role model for women entrepreneurs in other states. This is a fine example of economic empowerment of women.

Women's participation in the decision-making bodies has the potentiality to cleanse the political process of criminalization and corruption and ensure peace. There is a prevailing opinion that the increasing trend of mal practices and violence deter women from coming to public life. But the reverse also true. Women's participation will lead to the improvement of standards of public life.

Our development has not specifically focused on women. Therefore in spite of economic growth, enhancement of food-grain production and impressive strides in human development the male female ratio has not increased; rather it has declining incidence of rape, molestation, dowry killing female infanticide and domestic violence against women are increasing in alarming proportions. This is the result of inferiority status of women in society. We can reverse this by politically and economically empowering women.

Human Rights and Women

"Women Rights are Human Rights" expressed by the then UN High Commission for Human Rights Sergio Vioira demello, while speaking on international women's Day, 8th March 2003. In many countries, men and women are equal and that they enjoy the same rights and freedom. Human rights should apply to all people—man, women and children irrespective of caste, creed, religion and region. However, women often denied of their basic rights that form past of everyday life such as freedom of movement, access to education and participation in decision-making process. There are many barriers to equality between the sexes. Important factors including gender stereotyping violence against women, social and cultural attitudes, and discrimination laws and practices.

The Indian Government has set up several special institutions under different Acts of Parliament, to give effect to the constitutional provisions of human right of all persons including those of the disadvantaged and weaker sections of the society. These are the National Human Rights Commission (NHRC), the National Commission for Women (NCW), The National Commission for Backward Classes etc.

In India, it was late in 1993, National Human Rights Commission was established. More than half of the states have also set up state Human Rights Commission. Till 1970s, there was no case of human rights violations that have been lodged. Since 1993, the cases include human rights violations due to communal violence, caste conflicts, female foeticide, dowry deaths, domestic violence, attack or media. Though NHRC has got only investigating role, but had no power to punish the culprits.

For Indian women violence takes the form of foeticide, infanticide, dowry related murders, battering among others. What escalates violence is the widespread sanction for violence against women. Through such sanctions women are controlled and subjugated.

The common people should be aware of their basic Fundamental Rights and to be informed about various laws regarding these problems. In such times of strife and social conflicts, Human Rights professionals should emerge as can of hope to the helpless women victims of oppression. The different women organisations and the privileged women should strive for developing awareness in the minds of their part and illiterate sisters through mass media. About women's all round contribution to the family welfare so that man treat women with respect, understanding and equality. The struggle has to be carried on within caste, class, race, religion everywhere in which man women relationships figure and matter.

REFERENCES

1. Sidharth Das, *Women Empowerment in India, Orissa Review,* December, 2004, p. 56.
2. Braja Paikray, *Women's March to Equality, Orissa Review,* May, 2005, p. 55.
3. Dr. Jyotirmati Samantary, *Human Rights and Women: An Introspection Orissa Review,* January, 2005, p. 59.
4. Usha Narayana, *Economic and Political Empowerment of Women, Orissa Review,* January, 2002, p. 57.
5. Neera Desai and Usha Thakkar, *Women in Indian Society,* National Book Trust of India, New Delhi, 2001.
6. Leah Levin, *Human Rights Questions and Answers,* National Book Trust, New Delhi, 2001.

8

The Status of Women in India
A Managerial Look

*Dr. Sudhansu Sekhar Nayak**
*Dr. Anil Kumar Sahu***

Introduction

India, with a population of 989 million, is the world's second most populous country. Of that number, 120 million are women who live in poverty. India has 16 per cent of the world's population, but only 2.4 per cent of its land, resulting in great pressures on its natural resources. Over 70 per cent of India's population currently derive their livelihood from land resources, which includes 84 per cent of the economically—active women. India is one of the few countries where males significantly outnumber females, and this imbalance has increased over time. India's maternal mortality rates in rural areas are among the world's highest. From a global perspective, Indian accounts for 19 per cent of all lives births and 27 per cent of all maternal deaths. "There seems to be a consensus that female mortality between ages one and five and high maternal mortality rates result in a deficit of females in the population. Chatterjee (1990) estimates that deaths of young girls in India exceed

*Dr. Nayak., Lecturer in Commerce, Ramnarayan College, Dura-90, Berhampur (Orissa).
**Dr. Sahu., Reader in MBA, Berhampur University, Bhanja Bihar-7 (Orissa).

those of young boys by over 300,000 each year, and very sixth infant death in specifically due to gender discrimination." Of the 15 million baby girls born in India each year, nearly 25 per cent will not live to see their 15th birthday. "Although India was the first country to announce an official family planning programme in 1952, its population grew from 361 million in 1951 to 844 million in 1991. India's total fertility rate of 3.8 births per women can be considered moderate by world standards, but the sheer magnitude of population increase has resulted in such a feeling of urgency that containment of population growth is listed as one of the six most important objectives in the Eight Five-Year Plan."

Since 1970 the use of modern contraceptive methods has rises from 10 per cent to 40 per cent, with great variance between northern and southern India. The most striking aspect of contraceptive use in India is the predominance of sterilization, which accounts for more than 85 per cent of total modern contraception use, with female sterilization accounting for 90 per cent of all sterilizations.

The Indian Constitution grants women equal rights with men, but strong patriarchal traditions persist, with women's lives shaped by customs that are centuries old. In most Indian families, a daughter is viewed as a liability, and she is conditioned to believe that she is inferior and subordinate to men. Sons are idolized and celebrated. May you be the mother of a hundred sons is a common Hindu wedding blessing.

The origin of the Indian idea of appropriate female behaviour can be traced to the rules laid down by Manu in 200 B.C.: "by a young girl, by a young woman, or even by an aged one, nothing must be done independently, even in her own house". "In childhood a female must be subject to her father, in youth to her husband, when her lord is dead to her sons; a woman must never be independent."

Scope and Objective of the Study

The present study aims to highlight the social and economic status of women in India. Finally, a comparison is made on the position of women in India with world and developing countries of the world. Only secondary data are collected for the study purpose. So, all limitations of the secondary data are found in this study.

Analysis

The analysis of the data is made under the following important heads:

1. *Women are Malnourished*

Nutritional deprivation has two major consequences for women: they never reach their full growth potential and anaemia. Both are risk factors in pregnancy, with anaemia ranging from 40-50 per cent in urban areas to 50-70 per cent in rural areas. This condition complicates childbearing and result in maternal and infant deaths, and low birth weight infants.

One study found anaemia in over 95 per cent of girls ages 6-14 in Calcutta, around 67 per cent in the Hyderabad area, 73 per cent in the New Delhi area, and about 18 per cent in the Madras area. This study states, "The prevalence of anaemia among women ages 15-24 and 25-44 years follows similar patterns and levels. Besides posing risks during pregnancy, anaemia increases women's susceptibility to diseases such as tuberculosis and reduces the energy women have available for daily activities such as household chores, childcare, and agricultural labour. Any severely anaemic individual is taxed by most physical activities, including walking at an ordinary pace."

2. *Women are in Ill Health*

A primary way that parents discriminate against their girl children is through neglect during illness. When sick, little girls are not taken on the doctor as frequently as are their brothers. A study in Punjab shows that medical expenditures for boys are 2.3 times higher than for girls. As adults, women get less healthcare than men. They tend to be less likely to admit that they are sick and they will wait until their sickness has progressed before they seek help or help in sought for them. Studies on attendance at rural primary health centers reveal that more males than females are treated in almost all parts of the country, with differences greater in northern hospitals than southern ones, pointing to regional differences in the value placed on women. Women's socialization to tolerate suffering and their reluctance to be examined by male personnel are additional constraints in their getting adequate healthcare.

3. *Uneducated Women*

Women and girls receive far less education than men, due both social norms and fears of violence. India has the largest population of non-school-going working girls. India's constitution guarantee free primary school education for both boys and girls up to age 14. This goal has been repeatedly reconfirmed, but primary education in India is not universal. Overall, the literacy rate for women is 39 per cent versus 64 per cent for men. The rate for women in the four large northern states—Bihar, Uttar Pradesh, Rajasthan and Madhya Pradesh—is lower than the national average: it was 25 per cent in 1991. Attendance rates from the 1981 census suggest that no more than 1/3 of all girls (and a lower proportion of rural girls) aged 5-14 are attending school.

Although substantial progress has been achieves since India won its independence in 1947, when less than 8 per cent of females were literate, the gains have not been rapid enough to keep pace with population growth; therc were 16 million more illiterate females in 1991 than in 1981.

4 *Women are Stressed and Overworked*

Women work longer hours and their work is more arduous than men's still, men report that "women, like children, eat and do nothing." Women work roughly twice as many hours as men. Women's contribution to agriculture—whether it he subsistence farming or commercial agriculture—when measured in terms of the number of tasks performed and time spent, is greater than men. "The extent of women's contribution is aptly highlighted by a micro study conducted in the Indian Himalayas which found that on a one hectare farm, a pair of bullocks works 1,064 hours, a man 1,212 hours and a women 3,485 hours in a year."

In Andhra Pradesh, (Mies, 1986) found that the work day of an women agricultural labourer during the agricultural seasons lasts for 15 hours, from 4 am to 8 pm, with an hour's rest in between. Her male counterpart works for seven to eight hours, from 5 am to 10 am or 11 am and from 3 pm to 5 pm.

Another study on time and energy spent by men and women on agricultural work (Batliwal, 1982) found that 53 per cent of the total human hours per household are contributed by women as compared to 31 per cent by men. The remaining contribution comes from children.

5. *Women are Mostly Unskilled*

Women have unequal access to resources. Extension services tend to reach only men, which perpetuates the existing division of labour in the agricultural sector, with women continuing to perform unskilled tasks. A World Bank study in 1991 reveals that the assumption made by extension workers is that information within a family will be transmitted to the women by the men, which in actual practice seldom happens. "The male dominated extension system tends to overlooks women's role in agriculture and proves ineffective in providing technical information to women farmers."

Mapping Progress, states, "in the farm sector, the process of mechanization of agricultural activities has brought in tendencies for gender discrimination by replacing men for a number of activities performed by women and also by displacing the labor of women from subsistence and marginal households. Women are employed only when there is absolute shortage of labour and for specific operations like cotton-picking.

To supply food-processing industries being set up with foreign collaboration, there has already been a major shift from subsistence farming method of rice, millet, corn and wheat to cash-crop production of fruit, mushrooms, flowers and vegetables. This shift has led to women being the first to lose jobs."

A number of factors perpetuate women's limited job skill: if training women for economic activities requires them to leave their village, this is usually a problem for them. Unequal access to education restricts women's abilities to learn skills that require even functional levels if literacy. In terms of skill development, women are impeded by their lack of mobility, low literacy levels and prejudiced attitudes toward women. When women negotiate with banks and government of officials, they are often ostracized by other men and women in their community for being 'too forward'. Government and bank officials have preconceive ideas of what women are capable of and stereotypes of what is considered women's work.

6. *Mistreated Women*

Violence against women and girls is the most pervasive human rights violation in the world today. Opening the door on the subject of violence against the world's females is like standing at the threshold of an immense dark chamber vibrating with collective anguish, but with the sounds of protest throttled back to a murmur. Where there should be outrage aimed at an intolerable status quo there is instead denial, and the largely passive acceptance of the way things are.

Male violence against women is a worldwide phenomenon. Although not every woman has experienced it, and many expect not to, fear of violence is an important factor in the lives of most women. It determines what they do, when they do it, where they do it, and with whom. Fear of violence is a cause of women's lack of participation in activities beyond the home, as well as inside it. Within the home, women and girls may be subjected to physical and sexual abuse as punishment or as culturally justified assaults. These acts shape their attitude to life. And their expectations of themselves.

The insecurity outside the household is today the greatest obstacle in the path of women. Conscious that, compared to the atrocities outside the house, atrocities within the house are endurable, women not only continued to accept their inferiority in the house and society, but even called it sweet.

In recent years, there has been an alarming rise in atrocities against women in India. Every 26 minutes a woman is molested. Every 34 minutes a rape takes place. Every 42 minutes a sexual harassment incident occurs. Every 43 minutes a woman is kidnapped. And every 93 minutes a woman is burnt to death over dowry.

One-quarter of the reported rapes involve girls under the age of 16 but the vast majority are never reported. Although the penalty is severe, convictions are rare.

7. *Women are Helpless and Powerless*

Legal protection of women's rights have little effect in the face of prevailing patriarchal traditions.

(A) Marriage

Women are subordinate in most marriages. The position of women in northern India is notably poor. Traditional Hindu society in northern rural areas is hierarchical and dominated by men, as evidenced by marriage customs. North Indian Hindus are expected to marry within prescribed boundaries: the bride and groom must not be related, they have no say in the matter, and the man must live outside the woman's natal village.

In the south, in contrast, a daughter traditionally marries her mother's brother or her mother's brother's son (her first cousin). Such an arrangement has a dramatic impact on women. "In southern India, men are likely to marry women to whom they are related, so that the strict distinction found in the north between patrilineal and marital relatives is absent. Women are likely to be married into family household, near their natal homes, and are more likely to retain close relationships with their natal kin."

(B) Child Marriages

Child marriage keep women subjugated. A 1976 amendment to the Child Marriage Restrain Act raised the minimum legal age for marriage from 15 to 18 for young women and from 18 to 21 for young men. However, in many rural communities, illegal child marriages are still common. In some rural areas, nearly half the girls between 10 and 14 are married. Because there is pressure on women to prove their fertility by conceiving as soon as possible after marriage, adolescent marriage is synonymous with adolescent childbearing: roughly 10-15 per cent of all births take place to women in their teens.

The Article cites a 1993 survey of more than 5,000 women in Rajasthan, which showed that 56 per cent of them had married before they were 15. Barely 18 per cent of them were literate and only 3 per cent used any form of birth control other than sterilization. Sixty-three per cent of the children under age 4 of these women were severely undernourished.

(C) Dowries

Women are kept subordinate, and are even murdered, by the practice of dowry. In India, 6,000 dowry murders are committed each year. This reality exists even though the Dowry Prohibition Act has been in existence for 33 years, and there are virtually no arrests under the Act. Since those giving as well as those accepting dowry are punishable under the existing law, no one is willing to complain. It is only after a "dowry death" that the complaints become public. It is estimated that the average dowry today is equivalent to five times the family's annual income and that the high cost of weddings and dowries is major cause of indebtedness among India's poor.

(D) Divorce

Divorce is not a viable option. Divorce is rare—it is a considered a shameful admission of a woman's failure as a wife and daughter-in-law. In 1990, divorced women made up a miniscule 0.08 per cent of the total female population.

(E) Inheritance

Women's rights to inheritance are limited and frequently violated. In the mid-1950s the Hindu personal laws, which apply to all Hindus, Buddhists, Sikhs and Jains, were overhauled banning polygamy and giving women rights to inheritance, adoption and divorce. The Muslim personal laws differ considerably from that of the Hindus, and permit polygamy. Despite various laws protecting women's right, traditional patriarchal attitudes still prevail and are strengthened and perpetuated in the home.

Under Hindu law, sons have an independent share in the ancestral property. However, daughters' shares are based on the share received by their father. Hence, a father can effectively disinherit a daughter by renouncing his share of the ancestral property, but the son will continue to have a share in his own right. Additionally, married daughters, even those facing marital harassment, have no residential rights in the ancestral home.

Even the weak laws protecting women have not been adequately enforced. As a result, in practice, women continue to have little access to land and property, a major source of income and long-term economic security. Under the pretext of preventing fragmentation of agricultural holdings, several states have successfully excluded widows and daughters from inheriting agricultural land.

Suggestions

Various measures have been suggested for the improvement of the social and economic status of women as follows:

Table 8.1: Position of Women in India, World and Developing World

Social Indicator	*India*	*World*	*Developing World*	*Kerala*	*Sri Lanka*
Infant Mortality Rate. Per 1000 live births	73	60	68	16	17
Maternal Mortality Rate, per 100,000 live births	570	430	470	-	140
Female Literacy, %	58	77.6	70.4	86.93	90.2
Female School Enrollment	47	62	57	63	67
Earned Income by females, %	26	58.0	53.0	49.8	35.5
Underweight Children, %	53	30	30	-	38
Total Fertility Rate	30	2.9	3.2	1.9	2.1
Women in Government, %	6	7 5	-	9	
Contraception usage, %	44	56	54	56	66
Low birth weight babies, %	33	17	7	-	25

- As women receive greater education and training, they will earn more money.
- As women earn more money—as has been repeatedly shown—they spend it in the further education and health of their children, as opposed to men, who often spend it on drink, tobacco or other women.
- As women gain influence and consciousness, they will make stronger claims to their entitlements—gaining further training, better access to credit and higher incomes—and command attention of police and courts when attacked.
- As women's economic power grows, it will be easier to overcome the tradition of "son preference" and thus put and end to the evil of dowry.
- As son preference declines and acceptance of violence declines, families will be more likely to educate their daughters, and age of marriage will rise.
- For every year beyond 4th grade that girls go to school, family size shrinks 20 per cent, child deaths drop 10 per cent and wages rise 20 per cent.
- As women are better nourished and marry later, they will be healthier, more productive, and will give birth to healthier babies.

REFERENCES

1. Purushothaman, Sangeetha, 1998, *The Empowerment of Women in India: Grassroots Women's Networks and the State*, New Delhi: Sage Publications.
2. Ramalingaswami, Vulimiri., and Jonsson, Urban, and Rohde, Jon. "The Asian Anigma," *The Progress of Nations*, 1996. New York: UNICEF.
3. Tinker, Anne, 1996, *Improving Women's Health in India*, Development in Practice Series. The World Bank
4. Venkateswaran, Sandhya, 1995, *Environment, Development and the Gender Gap*. New Delhi: Sage Publications.

5. Vinayak, Ramesh, "Victims, of Sudden Affluence," *India Today*, December 15, 1997.

6. Das, K.K., *Current Problems in Indian Education*, Scientific Book Depot, Cuttack, 1984.

7. Nanda, S.K., *Indian Education and its Problems Today*, Kalyani Publishers, New Delhi, 1977.

8. Economic Survey, 2004-05, *Directorate of Economics and Statistics*, Orissa, Bhubaneswar.

9. Statistical Abstract of Orissa, 2005, *Directorate of Economics and Statistics*, Orissa, Bhubaneswar.

9

Orissa Gram Panchayat Act for Women Empowerment

A Milestone to Popularize National Population Policy and Literacy Mission

Surendranath Panda,
Advocate, Aska (Orissa)

God has created this universe. In this universe everyone is interested to live in an organized sector. Initially people were not leading their lives in an organized way. But as time passed people learnt to spend their time in an organized sector by creating laws for their welfare. Throughout the world people live in organized sectors. But, discipline has not been achieved in each and every sector. So, different laws are enacted to control the people and their illegal activities in the society.

After independence we adopted a democratic form of Government Our Constitution guarantees the fundamental rights and at the same time we are to perform the fundamental duties resulting the all round development of the country.

Different provinces of India differ on many aspects. To keep all these people in one banner respective provinces have created different enactments. As India has adopted a Democratic Form of Government the same principle is also applicable even to the small units of people. Orissa is a province of India. In Orissa people has tested the role of democracy as it is applied in the panchayat elections. Article 40 the Indian Constitution has given a wide scope to different provinces to take steps to organise panchayats. This spirit of creating panchayats can be well understood from Article 40 which is reproduced here for reference.

Article 40: The State shall take steps to organize village panchayats and endow them with such powers and authority as may be necessary to enable them to function as units of self government.

As per the spirit of Article 40 the Orissa province has enacted Orissa Gram Panchayat Act in the year 1964. This act has given a wide scope to the inhabitants of the village to participate in the Panchayat Raj System. Even in the Panchayat Act some amendments have been incorporated with a view to include all sections of the people to participate in the election particularly the schedule caste, schedule tribe and backward communities and women.

As per 73rd Amendment Act, of 1992 some new provisions were included in the Constitution. Those amendments provide Constitutional sanction to democracy at the grassroot level. The Constitution 73rd Amendment Act, 1992 has added a new part IX consisting of 16 Articles and the eleventh schedule to the Constitution. As per 11th schedule family welfare, woman and child development, social welfare, including welfare of the handicapped and mentally retarded and welfare of the weaker sections in particular of the Scheduled Castes and Schedule Tribes are included. Basing on the directives of the 11th schedule of the Constitution the Orissa Gram Panchayat Act was also suitably amended to check the growth of population as well as to raise the rate of literacy in the State. Sections 11 and 25 of the Orissa Gram Panchayat Act were amended in the year 1994 and new provisions were added to check the growth of population and to raise rate of literacy. Section 11 of the

Orissa Gram Panchayat Act prescribes the qualifications for membership of the Gram Panchayat.

Similarly, Section 25 of the Gram Panchayat Act prescribes the disqualification for membership of Gram Panchayat. Among other disqualifications the following provision is most important to check the growth of population in the State.

Section 25: Disqualification for membership of Gram Panchayat.

"(1) A person shall be disqualified for being elected or nominated as a Sarpanch or any other member of the Gram Panchayat constituted under this Act, if he:

××× ××× ×××

(v) has more than two children

Provided that the disqualification under Clause (v) shall not apply to any person who has more than two children on the date of commencement of the Orissa Gram Panchayat (Amendment) Act, 1964, or, as the case may be, within a period of one year of such commencement, unless he begets an additional child after the said period of one year."

××× ××× ×××

This provision has rightly implemented in Orissa in Panchayat Elections. In occasions where the members of the Gram Panchayat do not oblige this provision cases are being filed to declare their elections as void. In a case in between Basudev Sahoo Vrs Akshaya Kumar Pradhan and others reported in 2004 (1) OLR - 41 the Hon'ble Orissa High Court has given the observation which is reproduced here for better understanding of the provision.

The right to contest the election is neither a fundamental right nor a common law right. It is a right, conferred by a statute. At the most, in view of Part IX of the Constitution the right to contest election for an office of Panchayat may be said to be a Constitutional right—a right originating in the Constitution and given a shape by a statute. Thus there is nothing wrong if the same statute, which confers the same right to contest the election, also stipulates necessary qualification, without which a person cannot offer his candidature for an elective office and also provides for disqualification, which would disable a person from contesting or holding an elective statutory office.

Similarly, in another landmark judgment in between Rajkishore Dalai Vrs. Kalandi Pradhan and another published in 2005 (II) CLR 323 and 2005 (Supp.) OLR (NOC) 1115 the Hon'ble Orissa High Court has given the following observation.

The intention of providing the disqualification contained in Section (1)(v) of the act is to prompt the citizens to follow the family welfare/family planning norms and to save the nation from population explosion. The other underlying purpose is that persons holding Panchayat and local Board offices should act as role models for the society inspiring the people to follow their conduct in the matter of family welfare and family planning. The disqualification provision is thus meant for persons not adhering to the family welfare norms or flouting family planning programme. In other words, if a person deliberately beget more than two children and flouts the family planning norms and thereby offends socio-economic programme, he is to be disqualified under Section 25 (1)(v) of the Act XXX

Hindu Marriage Act, 1955 has also provided some norms for Hindu marriage. One of the important provisions is that no one should have a living spouse at the time of marriage. In other words Hindu Marriage is based on the policy of monogamy. This provision has also been included in Orissa Gram Panchayat Act.

A person cannot be elected as a Sarpanch or a member of Gram Panchayat if he has more than one living spouse. This principle is applicable to people of all religions. Though the personal law of Muslim provide for polygamy, still a

Muslim cannot be elected as a member for Gram Panchayat if he does not come under the purview of monogamy.

Further more the Orissa Gram Panchayat Act has also included a clause regarding the ability to read and write Oriya with a view to raise the rate of literacy in the State. Section 11 of the Orissa Gram Panchayat Act prescribes the same.

Section 11: Qualification for membership in the Gram Panchayat—Notwithstanding anything in Section 10 no member of a Gram Sasan shall be eligible to stand for election.

(a) ....

(b) as a Sarpanch or Naib-Sarpanch, if he has not attained the age of twenty-one years or is unable to read and write Oriya,"

In a case in between Suryakanti Mishra Vrs. State of Orissa and others reported in 2005 (Supp.) OLR-906 the Hon'ble Orissa High Court has given the following observation.

A plain reading of Section 11(b) would thus show that a candidate would stand disqualified if he/she is unable to read and write Oriya. This provision does not speak about education qualification of a candidate. The provision thus signifies that a person having no academic educational qualification is eligible to stand for election of the Gram Panchayat, if he is able to read and write Oriya. In other words, even if a person has educational qualification, but is unable to read and write Oriya, he would not be eligible to stand for election.

××× ××× ×××

Reading and writing Oriya as provided in the Section 11 (b) of the Act is not in accordance with any standard of academic education, qualification but capability to read and write. Obviously, that means that the persons filing nomination must have the capacity to read and write Oriya alphabets as well as "Yuktakhyars" i.e. the alphabets made on combination of vowel and consonants.

Thus Orissa Gram Panchayat Act is a landmark enactment as it ensures social justice in addition to democratic rights to the people of the State.

10

Women and Sexual Harassment

A Critical Issue in Woman Empowerment

*Premananda Pradhan**

India is rich country with an ancient civilization and a rich cultural heritage spreading over thousands of years. From our Vedas and epics we get the authentic information about women scholars like Gargi, Maitriyee, Mamta and Biswabara, women writers warrior etc. The Hindu scriptures gave a very high position to woman in family and social life. The wife was considered as "Ardhangini" of the husband, which meant that she constituted half of the personality of her husband.

Gone are the days when the poets only described the fair sex with a halo of romance, comparing them to the moon and the flowers. But, however, with these honeyed words of flattery, men succeed in reconciling women to their domestic confinement. They were gradually suppressed and finally neglected in the ladder of social development. They have been facing intolerable physiological, psychological, social, sexual and cultural problems. Hence, women have lost their freedom, identity and image in the society. Therefore, woman empowerment is the emerging issue in the context of women development. Empowerment is a multi-dimensonal process, *which* should enable the individuals or a group of individuals

*Premananda Pradhan, Research Fellow (U.G.C. Sponsored Major Project).

to realize their full identity and powers in all spheres of life. It consists of greater access to knowledge and resources, greater autonomy in the decision making to enable them to have greater ability to plan their lives or have greater control over circumstances that influence their lives and free them from the shackles imposed on them by custom, belief and practice. Empowerment of women also mean equal status to women. Conferment of improved standards of living and acquiring self-reliance, self-esteem and self-confidence.

Objectives of the Study

The main objectives of the paper is:

(i) Are women actually powerless?

(ii) To find out the factors which hinders their empowerment?

(iii) To explore who will confer them powerment?

(iv) To suggest some policy options.

Analysis

When we think about empowerment it makes us puzzle. When we think about power element, it is paradoxically very controversial. On the grounds of protection and self-reliance let us examine women empowerment. When she was a child she is protected by her mother and when she was adult, she is protected by her father and when she became grown up. She is married and protected by her husband. Now the question arises does a woman need further protection.

The second problem relates to conferment of powerment. The question is who will empower them. However, it is logical to say that empowerment comes from the existing power element with women.

Thirdly, a woman actually becomes powerless when she is deprived of getting freedom and challenges to build of her capacities like self-esteem, self-dependence in income, leadership role in decision making, self-confidence in the employment avenues. However, sexual harassment is the key factor which makes the woman powerless in the society losing her moral, dignity chastity and self identity and finally she becomes "voice less".

The following table depicts about the gloomy picture relating to sexual harassment of women.

Crime against women: The National Scenario

According to National family and Health survey, 1998-99, 21 per cent women India have experienced some form of violence since the age of 15 and 19 per cent have been beaten or physically manhandled by their husbands. Violence also has an adverse effect on the women's health, especially leading to unwanted pregnancies, miscarriages, low-birth-weight babies, maternal deaths and sexually transmitted infections, including HIV and AIDS. As such the gender based violence that women and girls encounter has gone up in recent years.

The following table below indicates the crime against women under the different sections of Indian penal code (IPC).

Table 10.1

Sl.No.	*Type of Crime*	*Population*		
1.	Kidnapping and abduction (363-373)	14877	15617	16351
2.	Rape (376)	14846	15330	15151
3.	Dowry death (302/304-B)	05513	06006	06975
4.	Torture (498-A)	35246	36592	41376
5.	Molestation (354)	28939	30764	30959
6.	Sexual Harassment (509)	05671	05796	08054
7.	Importation of girls for flesh trade	00182	00078	00146

Source: National Crime Record Bureau, Ministry of Home Affairs, Crime in India (Publications).

Table 10.2 represents the multifacets of social crimes against women with special reference to Orissa. It is evident

Table 10.2: Violence Against women Registered Cases of Orissa in the State Commission for Women

Nature of Cases	1993		1994		1995		1996		1997		1998		1999		2000-01	
	R.C.	D.O.	R.C.	D.O.	R.C.	D.O.	R.C.	D.O.	R.C.	D.O.	R.C.	D.O.	R.C.	D.O.	R.C.	D.O.
Dowry Death	115	22	190	53	172	100	182	35	188	803	148	108	111	295	138	54
Dowry Torture	226	13	655	85	672	322	906	73	896	1600	854	545	635	1195	630	361
Non-Dowry Torture	101	08	180	28	178	53	322	44	530	756	537	326	460	796	403	230
Eye Teasing & Kitnap	38	03	36	01	25	02	40	02	27	14	40	31	35	80	38	24
Rape	79	03	85	02	99	04	83	05	88	52	136	64	86	202	94	48
Suspected Death	68	17	64	22	89	34	87	10	74	380	73	29	46	133	46	36
Cheating Rape	14	-	70	-	60	04	90	06	155	69	133	71	117	208	131	62
Misbehaviour	45	04	113	01	139	08	191	12	210	103	242	95	145	363	126	59
Service Matter	21	-	42	02	37	03	33	02	42	27	59	26	48	92	40	13
Harassment	52	-	139	02	209	16	274	20	452	214	543	304	532	839	487	275
Land Dispute	15	-	42	02	37	03	33	02	42	27	49	41	37	56	51	24
Others	161	08	370	06	256	77	119	55	117	280	108	60	170	236	159	67
Total	935	78	1986	203	1984	644	2358	285	2838	4341	2934	1700	2431	4439	2343	1253
Annual Growth Rate			112.41		-0.10		18.85		20.36		3031		-17.09		-3.62	

Source: State Commission on for Women, Orissa. R.C.: Registered Cases D.C.: Disposed of Cases.

that crimes against woman is not confined to a particular region or state rather it is all pervasiveness.

In the aforesaid context, the following suggestions are opted to combat the situation and improve the status of women in the society.

1. Attempt should be made to increase the economic independence of women as that would give them higher status and they will have a voice in the important matters of the family.

2. Voluntary organizations and Government should run institutions for the care and rehabilitation of homeless and destitute women or those who are deserted by their kith and kin.

3. Progressive laws should be passed to fight against evil practices like dowry, discrimination against women, insult or harassment of women and other unhealthy social customs and traditions. Legal procedures should be simplified so that these laws could be implemented easily and effectively. Speedy justice must be provided to women who go to Courts of law seeking relief against rape, illegal divorce, desertion humiliation, torture or threat to their life.

4. Law alone cannot guarantee justice to the suffering women. There is the need for social awareness. Many women are not in a position to either seek justice in the Courts or even to protest against injustice either due to acute poverty, intimidation, fear of the evil-doer or apprehension of ruining their social image. The voluntary women's organizations should come forward to highlight the cases of injustice against women and should fight for the cause of women by creating social awareness. They should highlight all incidents in which women become the victims to the carnal desires of man or his brutal behaviour.

5. It is rightly said that God helps them those who help themselves. Nobody can protect the interests of another.

The women, should, therefore, organize themselves and fight for their own rights. They should assert their position in the society.

6. The media can play a great role both in creating awareness about women's problems and fighting injustice against them.

7. A real and meaningful fight against social prejudices and unhealthy practices and customs could be possible only when women help each other. In the case of dowry deaths and torture of the bride on the basis of dowry, it is noticed that very often the women members of the groom's family take the leading part. It, therefore, becomes imperative on the part of women to develop a consciousness of common interest in order to protect their rights and enhance their social status.

8. Top priority should be given to female education, wherever necessary special Schools and Colleges should be established for the women candidate.

Since Sexual harassment as the key variable under the study, it restricts women empowerment. A women faces the plight situations like unwanted pregnancy, socially under estimation, social isolation and miserable health conditions due to sexual transmitted disease like AIDS. Ultimately she reaches at the suicide stage. The discriminatory treatment between he and she violates the noble philosophy of empowerment. We should never forget the ideals Mahatma Gandhi writing in "Young Indian" in 1918, Gandhi said "Woman is the companion of man gifted with equal mental capacities. She has the right to participate in the minuest details of the activities of man. She has same right of freedom and liberty as he". So long as sexual harassment persists, women empowerment is neither possible nor desirable. It is possible only when the existing laws of the land will protect the women from the sex harassment and would confer their true legitimate rights and liberties.

REFERENCES

(i) *Kurukhetra*, Nov. 2005 Vol. 54, Women Empowerment in the Rural Context.

(ii) Unequal Treatment Towards Women and Gender Bias H.H. Das Key Note Address U.G.C. State Level Seminar, Nuapada.

(iii) Reports and Statistics GOI.

11

Gender and Economic Development
With Special Reference to Status of Woman in Orissa

*Dr. (Smt) Harapriya Patnayak**

It is impossible to think about the welfare of the world unless the conditions of women are improved. It is impossible for a bird to fly an only one wing Swami Vivekananda.

Arise and awake to the woman of the world for want of empowerment and for this they could have raise their voice for Equality, Dignity and Self respect.

In the present age when man is exploiting the possibilities of life in other planets and scientific and technological developments, they could have achieved total transformation of life, it is gross irony of the fact that woman are not being considered as equal partners with men in their various endeavours. The women folks have to lead a life of deprivations and sufferings and they become the victims of male chauvinism.

Gender refers to the rules, norms, customs and practices by which biological differences between males and females are translated into socially constructed differences between

*Dr. (Smt) Harapriya Patnayak Head Department of Economics Khemundi College, Digapahandi, Ganjam.

men and women and boys and girls. The gender perspective of developments means recognizing that women stand at the cross roads between production and reproduction, between economic activity and the care of human beings and therefore between economic growth and development.

Women constitutes 48 per cent of the total population of India. Their welfare and development has been a matter of great concern. In India the slogan of feminism and gender equality are still distant dreams as the issue of woman in our country are neglected issue.

This is also none all the more pertinent during this era of globalization since these issues are being sidelined. At the end of five decades of development, women continue to be marginalized and peripheralised from development activity.

India is a country with an ancient civilization and a rich cultural heritage spreading over thousand of years. From our Vedas and Upanishads we get the authentic information about women scholars like Gargi, Maitriyee Biswabara. The Hindu scriptures, gave a high position in family, society and state. The wife was considered as "Ardhangini" of the husband, which meant that she constituted one half of the personality of her husband.

Objectives

The basic objective of the paper is to throw light on persistence of gender in equality in India and Orissa. Despite various measures have been implemented to protect the women from unjust system operating to keep them in lower status. Discrimination on the ground of sex noticed from wombs of mother to death of women. To make an assessment on social, economic, physical and psychological hazards face by women and steps have been taken to combat such ills which not only help the women to raise their status but help our society to grow as a powerful race too. This chapter attributes Gender Economic Development specially to women in different aspects.

Gender Analysis

Sex Ratio:-Sex ratio is expressed as number of females per 1000 males. Sex ratio also responsible for the development of women. Some data of ratio of different important countries of the world given below.

Table 11.1

Countries of the world	*Sex ratio*
Russia Federation	1140
Japan	1041
USA	1029
Brazil	1025
Nigeria	1016
Indonesia	1004
China	944
Pakistan	938
India	933

Source: World population prospects (1998 revision).

Table 11.2: Sex Tatio of India and Orissa

Sensus Years	*India*	*Orissa*	*Gap between India & Orissa*
1901	972	1037	+65
1921	955	1086	+131
1951	946	1022	+76
1961	941	1001	+60
1991	927	971	+44
2001	933	972	+39

Source: Census of India Series-22 Orissa, Rural urban Distribution of Population, Director of census operation, Orissa.

From the above table it is revealed that Sex ratio of Orissa is higher than in India. In case of Orissa Sex ratio is declined after, first five year, plan i.e. 1951 but females are more accompanists to man in India.

Women Literacy and Education

Education is of great instrumental value in the process of economic growth and Development; Female literacy is highly essential to Economic Development. Access to education itself enables a girl to take independent decision in several matters pertaining to her own interest. She can ask for equal treatment in the family and the society, demand for equal rights and protest against any kinds of discrimination. Education of the girl child enables her to protest as against her early marriage, which is the root cause of her sufferings like ill health, malnutrition higher rate of infant mortality and even increased risk to the life as the mother.

In 1990 the UNICEF observed that "Education in the case of girls, is an expendable option and her own social status is reflected in her lesser, entitlement to care and attention. Her childhood years are crowded with domestic chores and the self-image that society creates for her in one of worthlessness, servitude and dependence." Female education is seen to be important in the process of lowering fertility and mortality. An educated and skilled worker force contributes to higher Economic growth unless women are educated; there is little scope for the socio-economic transformation of the society.

In order to analyse the literacy condition in our country as well as in the state of Orissa genders wise literacy rate female from 1951 to 2001 census figure presented in following table.

1951-71 literacy rate relate to population 5 years and above 1981-01 relate aged 7 years and above from 1981 Assam and 1991 Jammu & Kashmir excluded.

If we look in to gender wise education scenario of Orissa female literacy is lower than the males. It is also same in

Table 11.3: Literacy in India and Orissa

Year	India			Orissa		
	Persons	*Males*	*Females*	*Persons*	*Males*	*Females*
1951	18.33	27.16	8.86	15.80	27.32	4.52
1961	28.30	40.40	15.35	27.66	34.68	8.65
1971	34.45	45.96	21.97	26.18	38.29	13.92
1981	43.57	56.38	29.76	33.62	46.39	20.60
1991	52.21	64.13	39.29	49.09	63.09	34.68
2001	65.38	75.85	54.16	63.61	75.95	50.97

Source: Economic Survey.

case of India. Since from independence it is lower. This may be due to two reasons first girls dropout rate during upper primary stage might be more due to poor condition of household or lack of access to upper primary school. Secondly social constraints.

Table 11.4: Age Specific Enrolment Ratio of Students in Orissa

1995-96

Age Group	*Rural*			*Urban*		
	Male	*Female*	*Total*	*Male*	*Female*	*Total*
6-10	69	54	61	80	79	63
11-13	73	54	64	81	79	66
14-17	53	32	43	69	67	47
18-24	18	4	11	29	17	13

Source: NSSO (1998).

How ever Governmental Statistics with regard to the enrolment of Girls in the Schools present an extremely gloomy picture and the ground reality is still worse. Girls from more than half of the illiterate children in the age group of 5-9 years. The heavy dropout rates takes away from school more than half the girls enrolled in the school. The non-formal education programme has also lost its relevance due to the diverse local conditions in which the girl child is placed.

Table 11.5: Class wise Attention Rate (Percent) of Students in Orissa (1993)

Class	*Boys*	*Girls*	*Total*
1.	100.00	100.00	1100.00
2.	82.29	78.61	80.58
3.	78.18	72.62	75.64
4.	66.40	59.39	63.20
5.	53.44	46.71	50.14
6.	47.31	35.01	38.98
7.	34.71	32.61	36.47
8.	31.85	23.75	28.15
9.	29.48	21.88	26.01
10.	24.72	18.29	21.78

Source: NSSO.

Women and Healthcare in Orissa

The family in very sacred institution in India and women occupy very important position in family. The healthcare of women in also very important. Women all too often suffer ill health silently particularly when it is related to sexuality reproduction women through long years of socialization re-enforced by competing demands on their time and energy often do not acknowledge their own health problems. In Orissa the marriage of girls below 18 years may results in more births high infant mortality, and pregnancy complications etc. all results ill health, given to women than men. Healthcare given to female child. Then male child so. Measures should adopted in Orissa proper health care is given to women child.

Environmental Education to Woman

Environmental education research and awareness for women is vital. If we are to protect to future generation of plant and wildlife and build understanding and support for conservation of our nature. The tribal women follow old tradition Podu cultivation causing forest firing, unscaled cutting of trees, overgrazing and population explosion are the instant reasons resulting environmental deterioration of the area. Deforestation imbalances the meteorology fluctuating the seasonal thermometric readings rainfall, humidity and wind velocity. The National Forest Policy 1952 and 1988 suggest different measures and among these environmental education for tribal women is highly essential and given priority. Training programme should be conducted for improving local knowledge and skill of women. Involving women in voluntary organization and local level organization for creating ecological awareness and providing necessary technical know-how. Environmental degradation makes the life of the Indian women humanly impossible. Though they are the first and best managers of the natural assets They have an important positive role to protect and preserve the mother nature. Hence women's education is highly essential for active involvement in environmental protection and conservation of the natural resources.

Women and Labour

There is gender discriminates found in Orissa's labour market both on the social and economic front. Majority of the women workers in rural areas are engaged in agriculture, while urban women workers are primarily employed in unorganised sectors such as household industries trade, services + building construction works etc. In Orissa the study found that man spend 40-12 hours per week where as a woman spend 17.07 hours in SNA (system of national accounts) activities in the state. The rural woman spend 19.03 hours per week.

Woman carry greater burden of work in unpaid activities than men since woman are responsible for greater share of non-SNA work. In order to maintain the better social life in family woman perform various household activities like cooking, looking after children. Taking care of sick and aged person of family. Cleaning house hold utensils and house etc... which constitute 90 per cent of work the rest 10 per cent done by male member. Sometimes form the 10 per cent of work man also Forced woman to do some work. The role of women in household management is significant. In 2000 a study was made by a scholar and it was found that a working women in Bubaneswar Capital City of Orissa spend averagely 6.62 hours on an average per day on domestic work think of the rest work done by her in job work, so it is conclude that in labour field there is discrimination of women in Labours Economy Market.

Empowerment of Women

Nowadays gender empowerment has been recognised as a key improvements in the empowerment of women in country like India. Women empowerment includes:

1. Acquiring knowledge and under standing of gender relations and ways in which these relations may be changed. This can be achieved mainly through the reductions gender inequality in education levels increased literary of women removal of the old curricula that stereotypes women as only mother and wives.

2. Developing a sence of self worth a belief in ones ability to secure desire changes and the right to control ones life. There is need for reform in the domestic, political and other institutions that have been discriminating against women.

3. Gaining the ability to generate choices and exercise bargaining power. By acknowledging girls women's out put as an important contribution in the society as well as acknowledging that women's income is not a threat to men there the bargaining position for women can be enhanced starting from the household level to higher decision-making institutions like parliament .

Delivering the presidential address at a seminar on right to women in New Delhi the then chief justice of India justice

A.S. Anand said that Indian legal systems had adequate provisions to safeguard women's rights, but there was a need to properly implement them. "The Problem in not about the existence of Laws that safeguard women's rights, but about translating their dejure rights in to de facto ones" women empowerment would materialize and assume a concrete shape any if two key solutions are put to use wholeheartedly. First women should establish their own identity and respect their own individuality by believing in their capabilities and also by acknowledging the presence of her own species in relation to the society by being bold and determined secondly gender equality should be actualized. The destruction on one to the profit of the other would have adverse effect on the natural balance. The very issue of women's empowerment crops up because of man's refusal to view a woman as his other half with out which his individuality identity is incomplete.

Critical Appraisal

Women constitute one-half of the population in every Society and the society that ignores the equal rights of the women is an incomplete one and needs to be reformed. The meaningful transformation of the society is possible only when there is real emancipation of the women and they enjoy their rights in terms of equality with men. Mrs. Indira Gandhi, Mrs. Margarat Thatcher, Mrs. Golda Meir, as Prime Minister of India the U.K. and Israel respectively has proved that they take up highest responsibility of the state they could excel Men.

It will not be out of place at the end to suggest some methods for improving the status of women in the society.

1. Top priority should be given to the women education especially in rural and tribal areas. School and Colleges should established in Backward areas.

2. Progressive laws should be passed to fight against evil practices like dowry, discrimination against women, harassment of women and other unhealthy social customs

and tradition. Speedy justice must be provided to women who go to the court of law.

3. Voluntary Organisation and Government should nun institutions for the care and rehabilitation of homeless and destitute women or those who are deserted by their kith and kin.
4. Media also play a important role both in creating awareness about women's problems and fighting justice against them.
5. More and more participation of women in the policy-makings bodies and their emergence as social, culture and corporate leaders will not only focus the national attention on women problem but also help them in asserting their rights ands demanding equal opportunities and privileges.
6. William Henry says, "Nature gave women too much Power. The Law gives them too little". But in this millennium the law has started giving them more so various self-help groups (SHGS) were came together i.e. formed to empower not only the women but also for the family and community as a whole.
7. As said by Marx an India, "Women are the last to be hired and the first to be fired" to demolish this fact, general awareness should be created among women regarding their importance in the society, their Social Status, and legal rights etc. when they become more and more conscious of their identity, their very self has persuaded then to show their, mater in a male dominated society. This will expand their roles in the society.
8. Each and every woman has potentiality in her. Motivation should be given to bring out their potentialities. This will improve their status.
9. A real and meaningful fight against social prejudices and unhealthy practices and customs could be possible only when women help each other.

10. It is rightly said that God Help them those who help themselves. No body can protect the interest of another. The women should, therefore organise themselves and fight for their own rights. They should assert their position in the society. To day in all sectors of the Economy Women's concern have been flagged. But the challenge, lies in converting these into reality, in every field of economy there in gender discrimination.

REFERENCES

1. Das, Subrata, *Women's Status Myth and Truth, Social Welfare,* September, 1997, p. 23.
2. Reports of the National Committee on the Status of Women in India ICSSR, New Delhi, 1975.
3. Towards Equality: Report of CSWI, pp. 365-66.
4. Sharma Ursula, *Women's Work Class and Urban Household,* p. 150.
5. CSWI Report, pp. 1-10.
6. Malini Bhatta Charya, Women and Globalization, *The Hindu,* January, 4-2005, p. 15.
7. Employment Newspaper, 5-11 March, 2005, p. 2.
8. *Third Concept,* Vol 216, pp. 33-35.
9. *Vision,* Vol. XVIII, pp. 17-23.
10. Dr. Bina Sarma, *Socio-Economic Status of Women Contemporary India.* The Q uest for Equality, pp. 26-36.

12

Developments in Economic Empowerment of Women in India

A Study in Orissa

*Dr. Eswar Rao Patnaik**

Introduction

Economic development is the outcome of human efforts. Human efforts and the efficiency are the result of the status of the individuals, which they enjoy in a wider social, cultural, religious and political system of nation. Globally, there has been acceptance of a role for women outside the household. International efforts have created awareness among people regarding importance of gender equality of late national governments have initiated public policies for advancement of women. The Government of India has declared 2001 as women's empowerment year. Financial independence is an important step towards empowerment of women. The general assembly of U.N.O. adopted "Conventions on elimination of all forms of discrimination on women" on 18th December 1979 to enforce women's rights. World leaders have endorsed gender equality and empowerment of women as one of the eight millennium development goals at the millennium summit held in New York in 2000. An analysis

*Dr. Eswar Rao Patnaik, S.B.R.G. Women's College, Berhampur, District: Ganjam, Orissa.

of the, Human Development Report, 1995 reveals that, men's work in the marketplace is the result of join production and not solo effort. Further, if women's unpaid work were properly valued, women may emerge in most societies as major bread winners or at least equal bread winners (Anil Kumar Thakur, 2000).

Review of Literature

K. Tiruvenkatachari and S. Lakshmi have observed in their paper entitled "changing role of gender in economic theory", published in 77th I.E.A. conference volume, 1992 that, J.S. Mill (1969) had strongly pleaded for gender equality in respect of employment. Marxists, like Engels (1884) argued that, capitalism was responsible for restricting women from taking employment outside their housed. Faweet (1918) and Edgeworth (1922) have examined and theorised the concept of "Equal Pay".

Mincer (1974) and Polachek (1981) have developed the human capital explanation for gender inequality in wage payments. They have reasoned that, women have preference for certain stereotyped occupations. As these occupations do not require huge investment in acquiring special skills, they receive lower wages.

Becker (1985) pleads that even when men and women spend the same amount of time or market jobs, the women will be offered lower wages than men. Women had more of housekeeping responsibilities. So housekeeping would be more effort intensive. So, women spend more efforts on housekeeping and less on market jobs, even if they spend the same time as men on market jobs. This accounts for their paltry earnings. Easter Boserup was the first scholar to probe into the puzzle. Prof. Colin Clark's seminal work on the economics of housework evolves to approach the money worth of house work as a complement to national income measure. In a superstitious maledominated and orthodox society, women who are income earners for the family are considered as dependents without having no sizeable voice in the decisions of the family. It needs recognitions that, discrimination between genders in respect of employment and wages retards the productivity of the country.

The status of women is closely connected with their economic position which in turn depends on their rights, roles and opportunities for participation in economic activities. The year 1994 has recorded female participation rates at 50 per cent for all developing countries 46 per cent for industrial countries 50 per cent for Japan and 28 per cent for India (Anil Kumar Thakur, 2006). For females, work participation rate increased from 12.06 per cent in 1977 to 13.99 per cent in 1981.

It is striking to note that, the unorganized sector employs women 94, per cent of women workers include workers in handicrafts, village and cottage industries, daily wage earners and landless agricultural labourers. Analysis shows that, nearly 80 per cent of women workers are employed in the rural sector. Over the years, the number of female cultivators employed at country level has declined by 32 per cent, but the number of male cultivators has increased by 6 per cent. It follows that; women are losing control over land as a means of production. The per centage of female agricultural labourers in India has staggeringly increased by 43 per cent.

A perusal of data furnished by 1991 census shows that, agriculture is the predominant sector, that absorbs 58.43 per cent of women workers, as agricultural labours and cultivators, cereal production occupies a major area in the map of agricultural development, and this means that production of oilseeds, cotton, fruits, spices, fruits, vegetables and flowers have low priority. Animal husbandry, holds the key for women's development, next to agriculture. In the secondary sector, manufacturing of beedi, textile garments, and handloom works, provide sustenance for 0.74 million construction of roads, buildings and water ways seems to be next heroine in the drama of women's empowerment. Reference may be made of tertiary sector, in which educational services and domestic services engage a little over million women workers each and wipe out tears from their eyes. Laundry and dyeing have 0.7 million workers, trade in grocery and grain has 0.67 millions. Another 12 industry groups absorb more than 1,00,000 workers each but less than half a million.

Women intensive industries which have more than 60 per cent of workers are rearing of hens and ducks, cattle and goat rearing, manufacture of beedi, and matches, cashew processing, collection of minor forest produce, services, and coir manufactures.

Table 12.1: Work Participation Rates in Orissa

Year		*Females*	*Males*	*Persons*
1991	Total	22.77	51.61	40.09
	Rural	26.97	52.98	30.16
	Urban	9.19	48.92	
2001	Total	25.60	52.19	39.20
	Rural	30.90	52.60	41.90
	Urban	11.50	50.80	32.20

Source: Various census reports.

From the foregoing tables it is evident that, there has been an increase in the female work participation rate from 26.97 per cent in 1991 to 30.90 per cent in 2007 in rural areas in the state.

Employment does not mean wage employment alone, it also includes self-employment.

It is understood from the Table 12.2 that, the tribal dominant Koraput district has 1518 women depending on small scale industries for their survival. The district has 992 small scale enterprises which are managed by women. Analysts, observe that, the total number of women employees in registered small scale industries and unregistered small scale industries in the rural oriented, forest rich, Koraput district is 657 and 1056 respectively in 2001.

Table 12.2: Participation of Women in Management, Ownership in SSI Sector in Koraput District

Sl. No.	*Name of the District*	*No. of Women*	*No. of enterprises managed by Women*	*Percentage*
1.	Koraput	1518	992	65.32
2.	Orissa	38,233	33,274	87.03

Source: Development Commissioner, Government of India, SSI, New Delhi, Third all India Census of SSI, 2001-02.

Prof. J.K. Parida in his paper entitled "Women entrepreneurs in KBK Districts of Orissa" published in "Employment and Entrepreneurial status of women in Orissa" (edited by K.C. Patra Pottamundei College, Orissa) has emphasized that, women college entrepreneurs in Koraput region have the urge to become economically self-sufficient, to establish their own identify, to assure risks, to work hard, with tolerance, to achieve excellence, when they are involved, to become confident and once they involved, can be easily be motivated. The liability side of the balance sheet points to debits, like, socio-cultural barrier, low literacy level, lens nobility, low dynamic nature, unique mental setup and household responsibilities. They are yet to go from traditional value system. While advocating for the removal of a "One size fit to all" approach, he offers a policy framework for tribal women.

1. *They are illiterate:* jobs can be selected for which education is not a criteria.
2. *Not mobile:* They can select such a business, where mobility is not necessary.
3. *Risk:* Start from no risk or less risky ventures.
4. *Finance:* To suit their economic backwardness such activities be chosen, where small finance is needed, viz. Poultry, Pisciculture, Floriculture, Tea, Coffee, Goatery, Sheep, Pig rearing.

5. *Forest based:* Beekeeping charcoal, Leaf plates, Cups, Bamboo crafts, Tassar and Medicinal herbs.

6. Oil seeds, Cashnuts, Neem, Kusun Oil and Karanja.

7. *Technical:* Radio, TV, Mobile, Reparing shops, Watch, Ice-cream and Food processing.

8. *Small traders:* Grocery, Tailoring, Tea Stall, Betal Shop, Agarbati, Pottery, Serving and Candle.

9. *Food and beverage:* Jams, Kendu, Mahua, Mango Jelly, Palm, Wax, Lac, Neem, Honey, Soap nuts.

10. *Artisan:* Spinning and Weaving ropes, Mats Bamboo and working ropes, mats, Bamboo, Baskets, Woodcrafts, Glass and Ceramic and Tassor Sarees.

Self-Employment and Agriculture

The lack of ownership of land is a deterrent on agricultural development, as it robs the peasant of the needed incentives to affect improvement in land. Up to 1987, 24000, acres of land have been distributed among 16,574 landless families in the district to dilute concentration of land in the lands of a microscopic minority in the agriculture based district. Observation reveals pecuniary requirement is less.

Professionalism: Such professions be chosen, in which professional skills are not required or the skill, they possess is sufficient.

Marketing: Go for such business, where there is demand.

It is possible to state that the resources of Koraput district can be developed in the following areas.

1. *Fruits:* Banana, Coconut, Pineapple and Mango.

2. *Floriculture:* Rose, Tube Road, Marigold and Gladiolas.

3. *Spices:* Ginger, Chilly, Turmeric, Onion and Garlics.

4. *Pisciculture.*

5. *Bamboo:* Poor man's timber.

6. *Woods.*

7. *Coffee.*

8. Agromatic and medicinal plantation is possible due to forests.

9. *Sericulture.*

10. *Handlooms:* Rich cultural heritage of crafts.

Basing on the availability of the resources in the locality, initiation, support and development of enterprise can be accelerated in the following areas. Agro-based commercial farming, seeds vegetable, dry farming, lands were high lands not viable for cultivation and land records were not up dated. The use of organic residue of biogas in the production of crops, completion of ongoing irrigation projects, renovations of drainage cuts, timely weather forecasts may enhance crop productivity, to the advantage of women cultivators. The expensive nature of H.Y.V. seeds has compelled public authorities to introduce measures for supply of improved variety of seeds in mini kits to formers at subsidized rate of Rs. 1/- per mini kit. In the four year period from 1983-87, 70,000 mini kits of paddy were distributed among 25000 cultivating households of the district. These seeds refer to mung and soybean. The women cultivator's response to seed supply programme was dull due to their contentment with subsistence level of existence (income) so, the government of Orissa has introduced an action oriented programme the field visit system by V.A.W.S. and agriculture experts in 1977. Ram and Sirohi have estimated that a rupee invested in extension work produced a return of Rs. 17. To motivate the tribal and non-tribal cultivators of the district, the V.A.W.S. should not be casual in their duty, visit farmers fields regularly and commune with tribal in their language and may be equipped with audio-visual aids. With a view to enhancing the earning power of women, plan endeavour may be directed to motivate women farmers of the area to resort to grown profitable crops like Paper, Soybean, Wheat, Jute and Coffee. Vegetable production involving growth of vegetables, lie Onion, Cauliflower, Potatoes and Tomatoes may be resorted. The introduction of crop loan insurance scheme in 1986 was directed to stablise the income of farmers in periods of adverse monsoon. The farmers have to pay insurance premium at the rate of 2 per cent of loan assured for Kharif Paddy or Rabi Paddy computation of the per acre yield of Kharif Paddy in the next six years will settle the amount of insurance to be paid to farmers. Model farmers may also be educated up to high school level by government express, after selection of model farmers on merit basis. Roughly, 31.17-45 per cent of lands come under drylands in Koraput region. Dry land farming in its intensive approach seeks to create mini water sheds in the economy involving (a) addition of manure on farm once in every three years (b) mixed farming, crop rotation use of improved nods, and lower seed rate (c) Deep tillage and contour bounding. In its extensive approach, dryland forming involves substitution of water consuming crops by less water consuming crops.

Conclusion

To sum up, economic empowerment of women centers round reforms both inside agriculture and outside agriculture. The scale of endeavour may be raised to create 110 days of wage employment per women agricultural labourer, under E.A.S. and Sampurna Grama Swarajgar Yojana Schemes instead creation of 16-17 days of work in a year. The education level of tribals is 21 per cent in 2007, and they may be educated on sound and interesting lines to widen job opportunities in different sectors of the economy. As sound heal holds the key for effective functioning of women workers as productive workers Allopathy, Yoga and Homoeopathy may be tried in the areas. Micro credit by barks to marginal farmers, organized into groups (under self-help groups) may regenerate the degenerated economy.

Table 12.3: Number (in 000's) and Proportion of Main Workers by Industrial Categories and Sex-1991 (India*)

	Industrial	*Persons*	*Males*	*Females categories*	*%age of Females to persons*
	Total main workers (I-IX)	2,78,940	2,16,018 100.00	62922 100.00	22.56% 100.00
I.	Cultivators	1,07,143	85,610 (38.41)	21,533 (39.63)	20.10% (34.22)
II.	Agricultural Labourers	73,752	45,482 (26.44)	28,270 (21.05)	38,3% (44.93)
III.	Livestock Forestry fishing, hunting etc. and allied activities	5,306	4,298 (1.90)	1,008 (1.99)	19,00% (1.60)
IV.	Mining Quarrying	1,717	1,504 0.62	213 (0.70	12.41% (0.34
V.	Manufacturing Processing weaving and repairs	6,743	4,523 (2.42)	2220 (2.09)	32.92% (3.53)
	(a) in household industry	21,649 (7.76)	19,210 (8.89)	2,439 (3.88)	11.27%
	(b) in other than household Industry				
VI.	Construction	5,434	5,015 (1.95	419 2.32	7.71 (0.60)
VII.	Trade and commerce	20,818	19398 (7.46)	1420 (8.98	6.82% (2.26
VIII.	Transport storage and communications	7,843	7,639 (2.81)	204 (3.54)	2.60% (0.32)
IX.	Other services	28535	23339 (10.23)	5196 (10.80	18.21 (8.26

•Excluded Assam and Jammu Kashmir

Note: Figures in parethesis denote percentage contribution.

Sources: Census of India, 1991, Series-1, India, Paper-2 of 1992, Final Population Totals Brief Analysis of PCA, Office of the Register-General and census commissioner, Government of India, New Delhi.

Table 12.4: Selected Indictors of Concentration of Women Workers by Industry Divisions (All India)

	1987-88			1993-94			
	P.C. Workers	*Concentration*	*P.C. Workers*	*Concentration*			
NIC Description	*Male*	*Female*	*Ratio**	*Male*	*Female*	*Ratio**	
1	2	3	4	5	6	7	8
02.	Raising of stock	2.39	10.77	72.25	1.87	10.53	75.95
05	Forestry and logging	0.22	00.67	60.51	0.32	00.36	38.51
21	Manufacturing of Food	0.16	00.34	56.06	0.42	00.66	46.51
22	Manufacturing of beverages, tobacco and related products	0.47	0.55	65.43	0.11	00.08	28.79
25	Manufacture of jute and other vegetable fibre textiles (except cotton and coir)	0.05	00.06	42.80	0.08	00.19	58.33
96	Personal services all	0.73	01.46	0.86	53.50	00.12	07.30

Index

❑❑❑